walking in Scotland

First published 2009

Produced by AA Publishing
© AA Media Limited 2009

Published by AA Publishing (a trading name of AA Media Limited, whose registered office is Fanum House, Basing View, Basingstoke, Hampshire RG21 4EA; registered number 06112600)

Visit AA Publishing at theAA.com/bookshop

This product includes mapping data licensed from Ordnance Survey® with the permission of the Controller of Her Majesty's Stationery Office.
© Crown copyright 2009. All rights reserved. Licence number 100021153

ISBN: 978-0-7495-6301-1

A CIP catalogue record for this book is available from the British Library.

Managing Editor: David Popey
Layout and Design: Liz Baldin at Bookwork Creative Associates
Image Retouching and Internal Repro: Sarah Montgomery
Series Design: Liz Baldin at Bookwork Creative Associates for AA Publishing
Cartography provided by the Mapping Services Department of AA Publishing

A04132

Printed by Leo Paper Group in China

PAGES 2–3: The view over Cruachan Dam and Loch Awe from Ben Cruachan, Argyll
RIGHT: Woodland at Killiecrankie
PAGE 6: The Highland Fault Line Walk in Queen Elizabeth Forest Park, Aberfoyle

AA

walking in Scotland

Discover sandy beaches,

ancient cities, glistening lochs and

dramatic mountain scenery

Contents

This superb selection of walks introduces the themes and characters that define the beautiful landscape of Scotland.

Introducing Scotland

Almost half the size of England, yet with barely one-fifth of its population, Scotland is a country of huge spaces and mountains on a grand scale not found anywhere else in Britain. It is also a nation steeped in history, the violent conflicts with its southern neighbour only one strand in a fascinating story.

The Landscape

Scotland's western seaboard is littered with islands – some great, some tiny – and with vast fjord-like sea lochs which penetrate to the heart of the highest mountains. This is the crucible of what we now think of as the Scottish identity, and yet it is only a part of the story. In the south-east the borderlands have their own identity, their rounded, sheep-shaven hilltops and deep valleys producing many tales and a character and people very different from the swirling Celtic kilts of the west. The south-west, too, has its own stories, with its Celtic origins mixed up with Britons, Irish and Viking traditions.

Southern Uplands

The Southern Uplands stretch across the British mainland, forming a barrier between the Scots and the English, and hosting some of the most colourful and bloody chapters in Scotland's history. To the east, the high, rounded sheep walks of the Borders have always harboured proud families. In late medieval times they were the reivers, striking across England at any time to take cattle and pillage their impoverished neighbours. The Union of the Crowns put an end to this lawlessness, but their balladry lived on and was immortalised by Robert Burns, Sir Walter Scott and later in the stirring words of Hugh MacDiarmid.

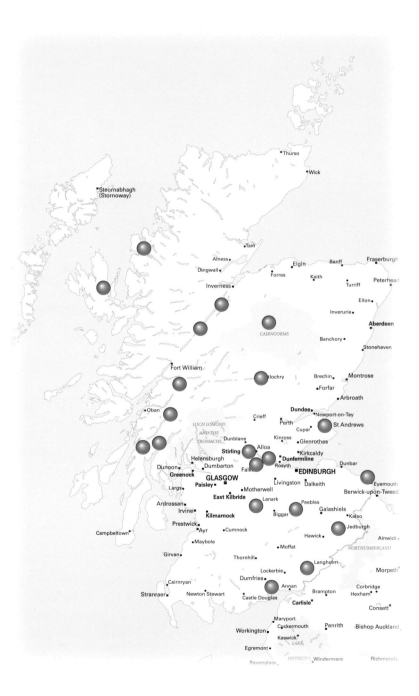

South-West Scotland

The south-west of the country was relatively peaceful, by comparision, until religious conflict in the 17th century tore apart families and culminated in the atrocities of the 'Killing Times', when troops loyal to the Crown were set against Presbyterian worshippers who refused to accept the Episcopalian church. Many hundreds died for the cause and their haunting memorials still stand in remote valleys and on dramatic shorelines.

The Central Belt

The incisions of the Forth and the Clyde are where most people actually live. This is where Scotland's own Industrial Revolution set the country on course to become the engine at the heart of the British Empire. From the Clydeside yards came the ships that kept a maritime kingdom playing on a world stage. The two great rival cities of Edinburgh and Glasgow vie for supremacy. Glasgow has the people, the football teams and the exceptional architecture of Charles Rennie Mackintosh and Alexander 'Greek' Thompson. Edinburgh has the political capital, the royal capital, the festival and the tourists.

Highlands

It is the Highlands that have come to define the myth of Scotland. Barely have you left Glasgow's northern suburbs and their breathtaking panoramas come into view. It is no coincidence that Loch Lomond is at the heart of Scotland's first national park. This long freshwater lake, edged by silver birch and Scots pine, almost captures something of everything you will see as you travel further north – the highest mountains, the red deer, the capercaillie shrieking its presence above the heather.

There are many differences in the Highland scene as you travel from west to east. The western mountains are jagged and rise fiercely from the glens. In the east they are less spiky but no less massive. On both sides of the A9, which serves as a convenient divider, you'll find deep valleys, sparkling lochs and remote beauty.

using this book

Information Panels
An information panel for each walk shows its relative difficulty, the distance and total amount of ascent. An indication of the gradients you will encounter is shown by the rating ▲▲▲▲ (no steep slopes) to ▲▲▲▲ (several very steep slopes). The minimum time suggested for the walk is for reasonably fit walkers and doesn't allow for stops.

Suggested Maps
Each walk has a suggested Ordnance Survey Explorer map.

Start Points
The start of each walk is given as a six-figure grid reference prefixed by two letters indicating which 100-km square of the National Grid it refers to. You'll find more information on grid references on most Ordnance Survey maps.

Dogs
We have tried to give dog owners useful advice about the dog friendliness of each walk. Please respect other countryside users. Keep your dog under control, especially around livestock, and obey local bylaws and other dog-related notices.

Car Parking
Many of the car parks suggested are public, but occasionally you may find you have to park on the roadside or in a lay-by. Please be considerate when you leave your car, ensuring that access roads or gates are not blocked and that other vehicles can pass safely.

Maps
Each walk in this book is accompanied by a map based on Ordnance Survey information. The scale of these maps varies from walk to walk.

map legend

--→--	Walk Route		Built-up Area
❶	Route Waypoint		Woodland Area
– – – –	Adjoining Path	🚻	Toilet
\\\|/	Viewpoint	P	Car Park
•	Place of Interest	⊞	Picnic Area
⌒	Steep Section	)(	Bridge

Through the Seasons

This far north you can expect snow on the higher peaks well into May. Unless you have experience or training in dealing with the different hazards posed by winter walking, it is advisable to stay out of the mountains at this time of year. At low level, particularly in the west, you will find it can be very wet and windy at any time of year – hill fog shrouds the mountains. Walking is a very popular pastime throughout Scotland but will you find the paths and tracks tend to be rougher than in England.

To avoid midges, which can make walking very uncomfortable in the north and west throughout the summer, get yourself a good insect repellent. Choose windier days and, if you are planning a trip, aim for the first few weeks in May or the middle of September. At these times you'll find the weather is often more settled, and you may be rewarded by clear skies, light winds and plenty of sunshine. Don't forget that daylight is relatively short at this latitude in the winter, so make sure you get an early start and carry a torch in your rucksack.

ABOVE: Loch Lomond

walking in Scotland

Discover sandy beaches,

ancient cities, glistening lochs and

dramatic mountain scenery

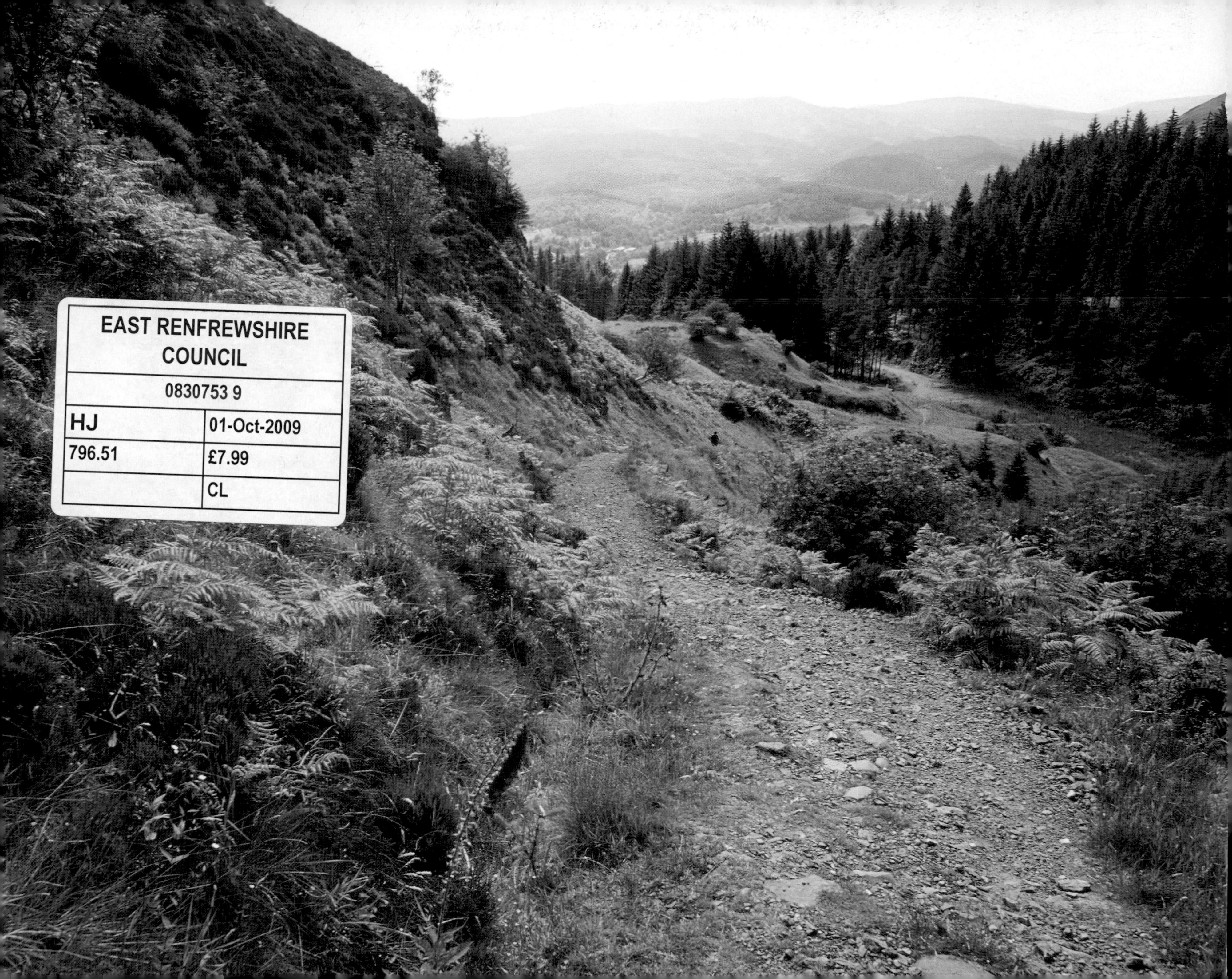

A pleasant walk around Loch Kernsary and down the Ewe — the country's shortest river.

Into Scotland's Great Wilderness

As you walk inland from Poolewe, you're entering one of the largest empty areas in Britain. Turn left instead of right at Kernsary Farm, and you can walk for two full days before you reach any road.

ABOVE: Gairloch village
LEFT: An array of autumnal colours in Gairloch

Great Wilderness

On the slight rise before Loch Kernsary, you get a surprise view right into the heart of this mountain wonderland. At the back of the view is A'Mhaighdean, the Maiden, Scotland's most remote mountain. It takes half a day's walk to get to this hill from anywhere. That walk will be along the edges of long dark lochs and under some very large crags. Beinn Lair has a quartzite cliff with an evil north-face gleam that's 3 miles (4.8km) wide, as big as the north face of Ben Nevis, but a whole lot less visited.

Behind A'Mhaighdean is An Teallach, called the Forge because of the cloudy vapours that stream across its semicircular ridge. That ridge has great lumpy towers to scramble round, 3ft-wide (1m) ridges to walk along and an edge that if you fall off, it will take about four seconds before you land on anything at all.

All this belongs to a gentleman from Holland called Paul van Vlissingen. In 1993 he signed an agreement with the Mountaineering Council of Scotland that first set out the principle of responsible access for all. Deer stalking restrictions would be only on days when deer stalking was actually taking place – a step forward when walkers were sometimes threatened with high-velocity rifle fire from August to February. The estate also undertook not to build any new four-wheel drive tracks. As a result, business here is carried out on foot, by boat and by pony. This Letterewe Accord became the foundation of the new century's access legislation.

LEFT: The shoreline near Gairloch village

Rights of Way

The paths used on this walk are, as it happens, on established rights of way. Even so, you'll notice a sudden change near the head of Loch Kernsary. The first part of the path has been rebuilt by the National Trust for Scotland, using their members' annual subscriptions. One new member pays for about 2ft (60cm) of path. At the edge of National Trust land the path repairs stop abruptly, mid-bog.

In Scotland, no one is obliged to build or maintain footpaths. The surprising thing, if you walk all of these walks, is how many people are doing it anyway. Paths in this book are looked after by charities such as the John Muir Trust, by Scottish Natural Heritage and Forest Enterprise, by private landowners in Argyll and Atholl, by regional and community councils and groups of ordinary walkers.

BELOW: Looking towards Loch Maree from the Poolewe

walk information	
➤ **DISTANCE**	6.5 miles (10.4km)
➤ **MINIMUM TIME**	2hrs 45min
➤ **ASCENT/GRADIENT**	250ft (76m)
➤ **LEVEL OF DIFFICULTY**	
➤ **PATHS**	Mostly good, but one short rough, wet section, 3 stiles
➤ **LANDSCAPE**	Moorland and loch side
➤ **SUGGESTED MAPS**	OS Explorer 434 Gairloch & Loch Ewe
➤ **START/FINISH**	Grid reference: NG 857808
➤ **DOG FRIENDLINESS**	Close control on moorland and tracks carrying estate traffic
➤ **PARKING**	In Poolewe, just up B8057 side street
➤ **PUBLIC TOILETS**	At start

walk directions

1 A kissing gate beside the public toilets leads to a path that crosses the Marie Curie Field of Hope to the main road. Turn left to cross the bridge over the River Ewe and then head all the way through the village. At the 40mph derestriction sign, there's a white cottage on the right. Beside it, a tarred trackway has a Scottish Rights of Way Society signpost for Kernsary.

2 Follow the track over a cattle grid to a new track that forks off to the left. After 50yds (46m), keep ahead on a path with a wall on its left. It passes through a kissing gate into Cnoc na Lise, the Garden Hill. This has been replanted as a community wood with oak and birch trees. Another kissing gate leads out of the young wood. The good, reconstructed path runs through gorse and then under a low-voltage power line. It crosses a low spur to a fine view of Loch Kernsary and the remote, steep-sided hills of the Great Wilderness, then goes over a stream to the loch side.

3 The path follows the left-hand shore of the loch, passing through patches of birch scrub. After a stile, near the loch head, it suddenly deteriorates, becoming a braided trod of boulder and bog. Once past the loch head, slant to the left down a meadow to find a footbridge under an oak tree. Head up, with a fence on your right, to join a track beside Kernsary Farm.

4 Turn right, through a gate. Follow the track past the farm, to a culvert crossing of the Kernsary River. This becomes a ford only after heavy rain. If needed, you will find a footbridge 70yds (64m) upstream. After crossing, turn right on a smooth track. The new track bears left, away from Loch Kernsary towards the hollow containing Loch Maree. After the bridge over the Inveran River is a gate with a ladder stile. Signs welcoming responsible walkers (and even cyclists) reflect the principles of the Letterewe Accord. Soon

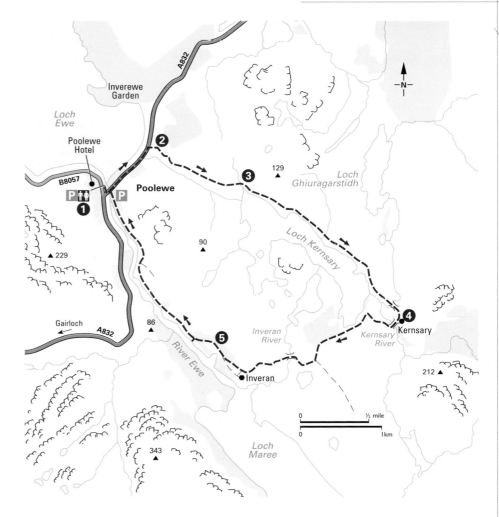

come the first views of Loch Maree. The driveway of Inveran House joins from the left and the track starts being tarred.

5 At a sign, 'Blind Corners', a green track on the left leads down to the point where the narrow loch imperceptibly becomes a wide river. Return to the main track and follow it above and then beside the River Ewe. It reaches Poolewe just beside the bridge.

A coastal walk to a raised beach called the Bile, then returning by way of Ben Chracaig.

Seeing Sea Eagles at Portree Bay

Portree is the capital of Skye, and its colour-washed houses set around the harbour arepleasing on the eye. While walking beside Portree Bay, keep at least one eye looking out to sea. You may spot the results of what has been described as Britain's greatest ever conservation story.

ABOVE: White-tailed sea eagle
LEFT: Loch Portree with the houses of Portree scattered on the far shores

Sea Eagle Story

The last sea eagle in Scotland died on Skye in the early 1900s. Like all large raptors, it was shot at by shepherds and gamekeepers. An attempt to reintroduce them in 1959 failed. In 1975, a secret RAF mission flew four young birds from Norway to the island of Rum. Over the next ten years, they were joined by 80 more. Today, about a dozen pairs are nesting here, with a total population of around 100 spread up along the western coast and the Hebrides.

In Gaelic it is called 'iolaire suil na greine' – the eagle with the sunlit eye – as its eye is a golden colour. In English it's also called the white-tailed eagle, the white-tailed fish eagle and the European sea eagle; it hasn't been back here long enough to finalise its name. Its nickname is the 'flying barn door' because it's so big, but it's not a heavy bird. Even with its 8ft (2.4m) wingspan, it weighs in at just 7lb (3kg). The sea eagle nests in cliffs. One nest, with an RSPB hide, is at Loch Frisa on Mull, another is here at Portree. The Aros visitor centre has a closed-circuit TV camera trained on the nest, and the Portree fishermen have taken to throwing seafood to the birds outside the bay. The eagle feeds by snatching fish out of the sea – but even more spectacular is its mating display, when the two birds soar and cartwheel high above the water.

Was that an Eagle?

The first few eagles you think you see are almost certainly buzzards. When you see a real eagle, and even though you can't tell how far away it is, you'll know it for what it is. It's four times the size of a buzzard and its wingbeats are slow and powerful. That's when it isn't gliding from one horizon to the other apparently without moving a feather. The sea eagle is even bigger than the golden one, and has a white tail – but so does a young golden eagle. However, if the eagle is flying over the sea, and especially if it's over the sea at Portree, then it's a sea eagle.

Naturalists believed that the bird's main problem would be the golden eagle, which during the years of extinction had taken over the nest sites. But sadly, the real enemy is still humans. In 2000, and despite a 24-hour guard, thieves took the two eggs from the Mull pair.

RIGHT: Colour-washed houses around Portree harbour, surrounded by trees

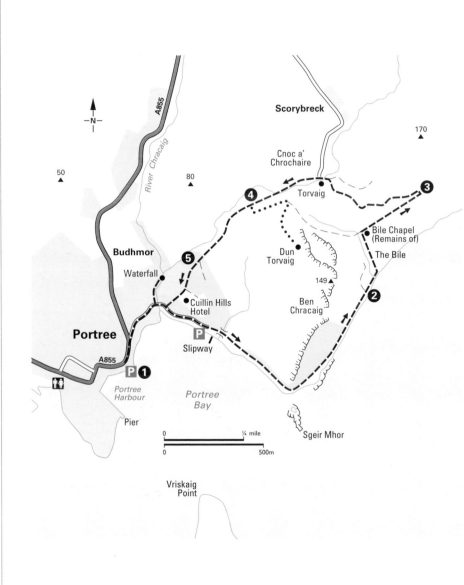

walk information

➤ **DISTANCE**	6.5 miles (10.4km)
➤ **MINIMUM TIME**	1hr 15min
➤ **ASCENT/GRADIENT**	459ft (140m) ▲▲▲
➤ **LEVEL OF DIFFICULTY**	🚶🚶🚶
➤ **PATHS**	Smooth, well-made paths, farm track, 3 stiles
➤ **LANDSCAPE**	Views across Minch from wooded coast and hill above
➤ **SUGGESTED MAPS**	OS Explorer 409 Raasay, Rona & Scalpay or 410 Skye – Portree & Bracadale
➤ **START/FINISH**	Grid reference: NG 485436
➤ **DOG FRIENDLINESS**	Dogs on lead through farmland, scoop poop on shore path
➤ **PARKING**	On A855 (Staffin Road) above Portree Bay. Another small parking area near slipway
➤ **PUBLIC TOILETS**	Town centre, just off village square

walk directions

1 Turn off the main A855 on to a lane signed 'Budh Mor', to walk down to the shoreline and then continue to a small parking area. A tarred path continues along the shore past a slipway. After a footbridge, it passes under hazels which show the typical ground-branching habit of bushes formerly coppiced – cut back every seven years for firewood. The path passes below a viewpoint with flagpoles and then rounds the headland to reach the edge of a level green field called The Bile.

2 A wall runs up the edge of The Bile. A sign points up left for Scorybreck but ignore it and go through a small gate ahead. A rough path leads into the corner of The Bile field. Go up its left edge and turn across its top, to a stile just

RIGHT: The harbour at Portree, Skye

above a field gate. Cross the top of the next field on an old green path, to a stile at its corner.

3 You'll see a track just beyond. Turn sharp left, up the track. At the top it passes through two gates to reach a stony road just to the right of Torvaig. Turn left past the house and cross the foot of a tarred road into a gently descending track. It runs down between two large corrugated sheds and then through to a gate with a stile.

4 The grassy path ahead leads down into Portree, but you can take a short, rather rough, diversion to Dun Torvaig (an ancient fortified hilltop) above. For the dun, turn left along the fence, and left again on a well-made path above. It leads to a kissing gate above the two sheds. Turn sharp right along the fence for a few steps, then bear left around the base of a small outcrop and head straight up on a tiny path to the dun. Remnants of dry-stone walling can be seen around the summit. Return to the well-made path, passing above Point 4 to join the wall on the right. The path leads down under goat willows into a wood where it splits; stay close to the wall.

5 At the first houses (The Parks Bungalow 5), keep downhill on a tarred street. On the left is the entrance to the Cuillin Hills Hotel. A few steps later, fork right on to a stony path. At the shore road, turn right across a stream and at once right again on a path that runs up for 60yds (55m) to a craggy little waterfall. Return to the shore road and turn right to the walk start.

*Overlooking Loch Ness and past
the home of a different monster, the
Beast of Boleskine.*

Farigaig Forest and Loch Ness

With so many fine sights in Scotland, it's a shame that such large numbers of people take the trouble to see one that doesn't exist. The first encounter with the Loch Ness monster was back in the 6th century AD, when St Columba was crossing the River Ness. One of his companions was attacked by a water beast. When the saint ordered it to go away, it did. The onlookers, pagan barbarians whose friend had already been eaten, promptly converted to Christianity.

ABOVE: *Wild flowers growing at Loch Ness*
RIGHT: *Urquhart Castle on Loch Ness*

The account was set down 100 years later by Adomnan, an abbot of Iona. It sounds suspiciously like an earlier incident from the life of a different holy man, St Martin of Tours, and also like a story about how Christianity took over a site where human sacrifice had been offered to a river god.

Later confirmation came during the Lisbon earthquake of 1755. A shock wave, freakishly magnified along Loch Ness, sent breakers crashing against the shore at Fort Augustus – clearly Columba's monster was still down there disturbing the water.

The Beast of Boleskine

Authentic sightings of a rather different monster did, however, take place in the early 1900s. Finding it fashionable to be Scottish, Alexander Crowley changed his name to Aleister and bought the nearby hall to become the Laird of Boleskine. In his time, he was known as 'The Beast of Boleskine', the 'wickedest man alive'. He identified himself with the Great Beast described in the final book of the Bible, the seven-headed monster that was to battle with the angels at the end of time.

In pursuit of his precept 'do what thou wilt shall be the whole of the law', he debauched minor film stars when given the opportunity, betrayed his friends and became an alcoholic and heroin addict. At Boleskine, as he studied his magical books, the sky darkened at midday so candles had to be lit, and the lodge keeper went mad.

We might take the darkening of the sky as a normal Scottish summer raincloud, but we can still see the rowan trees his neighbours planted to protect themselves from his dangerous magical influence.

RIGHT: Visiting the ruins of Urquhart Castle, Loch Ness

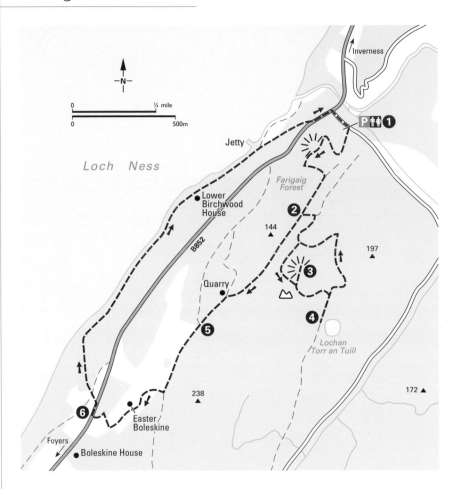

walk information	
➤ **DISTANCE**	4.25 miles (6.8km)
➤ **MINIMUM TIME**	2hrs 15min
➤ **ASCENT/GRADIENT**	700ft (213m) ▲▲▲
➤ **LEVEL OF DIFFICULTY**	🚶🚶🚶
➤ **PATHS**	Waymarked paths and tracks, no stiles
➤ **LANDSCAPE**	Hillside of mixed woodland
➤ **SUGGESTED MAPS**	OS Explorer 416 Inverness, Loch Ness & Culloden
➤ **START/FINISH**	Grid reference: NH 522237
➤ **DOG FRIENDLINESS**	Keep on lead for short stretch past Easter Boleskine
➤ **PARKING**	Forest Enterprise car park
➤ **PUBLIC TOILETS**	At start

RIGHT: Sunset on the shores of Loch Ness

2 Turn up left on a footpath with more yellow waymarkers. The path has a low, heavily mossed wall alongside as it bends up to a higher forest road. Turn right and walk for about 150yds (137m) until you reach a sharp left-hand bend. Turn off right here, on a small footpath through an area of small self-seeded trees, then go steeply up to the left underneath mature trees. At the top, bear left along a little ridge, dropping gently downhill to a fine viewpoint.

3 Return for 100yds (91m) and bear left down the other side of the ridge. The path now descends steeply until it reaches a forest road. A sign indicates Lochan Torr an Tuill, near by on the left, with a picnic table.

4 Return along the forest road, past where you joined it. It climbs gently and then descends to the sharp right bend where you turned off earlier – the waymarker says 'to Carpark' on the side now facing you. After 150yds (137m),

walk directions

1 From the car park follow yellow waymarkers uphill near a stream. After 100yds (91m), a path on the right has a yellow-top waymarker. After a bench, the path contours briefly then turns up left, to a higher viewpoint. It then turns back sharply right and descends on earth steps through a little crag to a forest road. Turn right for 200yds (183m).

at another 'to Car Park' waymarker, turn left down the path with the low mossed wall to the forest road below (Point 2). Turn left, past a red/green waymarker. The track kinks left past a quarry.

5 Where the main track bends right, downhill, keep ahead on a green track with a red/green waymarker. It emerges from the trees at a signpost. Follow this down to the right towards Easter Boleskine house. Green waymarkers indicate a diversion to the left of the house, to join its driveway track below. Follow this down to the B852.

6 Turn right for 50yds (46m). Below the left edge of the road is a tarred track. Turn down a faint path between the trees to cross this track, with a blue waymarker leading into a clearer path beyond. This passes down to the right of electricity transformers. At the foot of the slope, the main path bears right with a blue waymarker. It runs above the loch shore and joins a gravel track just below Lower Birchwood House. At a tarmac turning circle, an overgrown jetty on the left is great for monster-watchers. The tarred lane ahead leads up to the B852, with the car park just above on the right.

Following cattle thieves and drovers to the lochan used by the fairies for their laundry.

The Pass of Ryvoan and the Thieves' Road

The Pass of Ryvoan has all the atmosphere of a classic Cairngorm through-route. It's a scaled down version of the famous and fearsome Lairig Ghru that cuts through the Cairngorm range southwards from Aviemore. You pass from the shelter of the forest to a green lochan, trapped between two high and stony mountainsides. Once through the narrow gap, you'll find wide moors and a ring of peaks around the horizon.

ABOVE: Loch Morlich, with the Cairngorms in the background
LEFT: Loch Morlich, Aviemore

Thieving Ways

Ryvoan marked the exit of the Thieves' Road that ran out of Rannoch and Lochaber by secret ways through the Rothiemurchus Forest. The MacDonalds of Glen Coe used to come raiding here in the 17th century, as did Clan Cameron from Loch Eil near Fort William. Once through the pass, they could take their pick from the rich lands of Moray and Aberdeenshire. In more settled times, the raiding chieftains became landlords, and their rents were paid in the small black cattle of the glens. Every autumn, the drove herds assembled for their long walk to the markets of Falkirk, Perth and northern England.

The Old Drove Road

The drovers used the same road as their thieving grandfathers, but once through the pass they turned sharp right across the flank of the mountain. The Lairig an Lui, the Pass of the Calves, crosses the dangerous ford of the Avon and runs down Glen Derry to Braemar. It's 30 miles (48km) to the next grazing and shelter – two full days for the drove. Overnight the cattle would snatch some grazing from the rough grasses, while the drovers cooked their oatmeal and potatoes, before rolling themselves in their woollen plaids on a bed of heather. As late as 1859, Queen Victoria found the Lairig path torn up by hooves and scented with fresh cow pats.

The Sithe and Others

Lochan Uaine means 'Green Loch'. Some say the green colour is caused by flecks of mica. Others claim that it's where the fairies wash their green garments. The Highland fairies, the Sithe (pronounced 'Shee'), don't dance around with wands and grant you wishes. They are touchy and vengeful, and if you meet one it is best to address him politely in good Gaelic. Precautions you can take are to avoid wearing green, which is known to annoy them, and never to address your friends by name while under the trees.

The Bodach Lamh-dearg is a spectre who appears wrapped in a grey plaid with one bloodstained hand, challenging passers-by to a fight and leaving their bodies for the foxes. Big Donald, the King of the Fairies, lived beside Loch Morlich.

PREVIOUS PAGE AND LEFT: Loch Morlich, with the Cairngorms in the background

walk information

➤ **DISTANCE**	5 miles (8km)
➤ **MINIMUM TIME**	2hrs 15min
➤ **ASCENT/GRADIENT**	400ft (122m)
➤ **LEVEL OF DIFFICULTY**	
➤ **PATHS**	Smooth tracks, one steep ascent, no stile
➤ **LANDSCAPE**	Views over Rothiemurchus Forest to Cairngorm
➤ **SUGGESTED MAPS**	OS Explorer 403 Cairn Gorm & Aviemor
➤ **START/FINISH**	Grid reference: NH 980095
➤ **DOG FRIENDLINESS**	Off lead but under close control
➤ **PARKING**	Bridge just south of Glenmore village
➤ **PUBLIC TOILETS**	Glenmore village

walk directions

1 Head upstream on a sandy track to the left of the river. Interpretation signs explain the flowers of the forest you may come across, many of which are ferns and mosses. After 550yds (503m), turn left on a wide smooth path with blue/yellow waymarkers. Ahead is a gate into Glenmore Lodge rifle range; here the path bends right, to a wide gravel track.

2 Turn right, away from Glenmore Lodge, to cross a concrete bridge into the Caledonian Reserve. Immediately keep ahead on a smaller track (marked by a blue waymarker) as the main one bends right. The track narrows as it heads into the Pass of Ryvoan between steep wooded slopes of

pine, birch and scree. At this, the most scenic part of the route, a path turns left, with a blue waymarker, which you take in a moment. Just beyond this, steps on the right lead down to Lochan Uaine. Walk round to the left of the water on the beach. At the head of the loch a small path leads back up to the track. Turn sharp left, back to the junction already visited; now turn off to the right on to the narrower path with the blue waymarker.

3 This small path crosses some duckboard and heads back down the valley. Very soon it starts to climb steeply to the right, up rough stone steps. When it levels off the going is easier, although it's still narrow, with tree roots. The path reaches a forest road at a bench and a waymarker.

4 Continue to the left along the track. After a clear-felled area with views, the track re-enters trees and slopes downhill into Glenmore village. Just above the main road turn right, through a green barrier, to reach Glenmore Visitor Centre. Pass through its car park to the main road.

5 Cross to Glenmore shop. Behind a post-box, steps lead down to the campsite. Pass along its right-hand edge to a path into woods. Head left across a footbridge to the shore of Loch Morlich and follow the beaches until another river blocks the way. Turn left along the river bank. Ignore a footbridge, but continue on the wide path with the river on your right. Where the path divides, the smaller branch continues beside the river through bushes to the car park.

Extending the Walk

In good weather you can continue through the Pass of Ryvoan. Return to Glenmore by taking a hill path from the bothy, over the summit of Meall a' Bhuachaille and then down through the Coire Chondlaich.

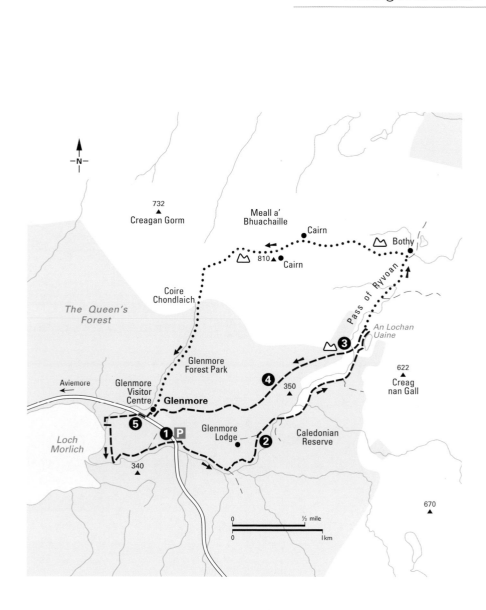

Above the Great Glen on the road the English built and Bonnie Prince Charlie marched over.

Up and Down the Corrieyairack

The most striking feature of Scotland's geography is the 2,000ft (610m) deep Great Glen. It runs perfectly straight from Fort William to Inverness as if a giant ploughshare had been dragged across the country. This walk allows you to explore a small but significant section of it.

ABOVE: *Looking down the Great Glen towards the Caledonian Canal and Loch Oich*
RIGHT: *The mountains of Stob A'Ghrianain and Beinn Bhan rise from the Great Glen*

Scotland's San Andreas

Around 400 million years ago, the northern part of Scotland slipped 65 miles (105km) to the left. Looking across from Corrieyairack you'd have seen ground that's now the Island of Mull. The Great Glen represents a tear-fault, similar to the San Andreas Fault in California, but no longer active, so that there isn't going to be any Fort Augustus Earthquake. Where two ground masses slide past each other, the rock where they touch is shattered. Rivers and glaciers have worn away this broken rock to make the striking valley.

Wade's Ways

After the uprising of 1715, General Wade became the military commander of Scotland. He constructed and repaired forts along the Great Glen at Fort William, Fort Augustus and Inverness, as well as at Ruthven on the present A9 and Glenelg. To link them, he built 260 miles (around 418km) of roads across the Highlands. The most spectacular of these was the one through the Corrieyairack Pass, rising to 2,500ft (762m) to link the Great Glen with the Spey. The construction was little changed since Roman times. Large rocks were jammed together into a firm bed, up to 15ft (4.5m) wide, and then surfaced with smaller stones and gravel packed down. Modern path-builders know that however well you build it, if it's got water running down it, it turns into a stream. Wade paid particular attention to drainage. The 500 soldiers working through the summer of 1731 got a bonus of 6d a day – about £5 in today's money – and celebrated its completion with a barbecue of six oxen.

The chieftains worried that the roads would soften their people, making them unfit for raids across rough country. But they soon came to appreciate the convenience. 'If you'd seen these roads before they were made, You'd lift up your hands and bless General Wade.'

And when Prince Charles Stuart landed 14 years later, it was the Jacobite army that marched triumphantly across the Corrieyairack. At the Speyside end of the pass, a small and ill-prepared force under General John Cope fled before him into England. And a new Wade rhyme was inserted, temporarily, into the National Anthem itself: 'God grant that Marshal Wade, May by Thy mighty aid, Victory bring, May he sedition hush, and like a torrent rush, Rebellious Scots to crush, God save the King.'

walk directions

1 A track leads round to the left of the burial ground to meet a minor road. Turn right for about 0.25 mile (400m) to the foot of a rather rubbly track signposted for the Corrieyairack Pass. After some 50yds (46m) the track passes through a gate, getting much easier, and, soon, the right of way joins a smoother track coming up from Culachy House.

2 After another 0.25 mile (400m), a gate leads out on to the open hill. About 350yds (320m) further on, the track passes under high-tension wires. At once bear left across a grassy meadow. As this drops towards a stream, you will see a green track slanting down to the right. Bear left off the track to pass the corner of a deer fence, where a small path continues down to the stream. Cross and turn downstream on an old grassy track. It recrosses the stream and passes under the high power line to a bend with a sudden view across deep and wooded Glen Tarff.

3 Turn right across a high stone bridge. A disused track climbs through birch woods then, as a terraced shelf, across the high side of Glen Tarff. A side stream forms a wooded re-entrant ahead. The old track contours in to this and crosses below a narrow waterfall – the former bridge has now disappeared.

4 Contour out across the steep slope to pick up the old track as it restarts. It runs gently uphill to a gateless gateway in a fence. Turn up the fence to another gateway, 150yds (137m) above. Here turn left for 20yds (18m) to the brink of another stream hollow. (Its delightful Gaelic name – Sidhean Ceum na Goibhre – means 'Fairy Goat-step'.) Don't go into this, but turn uphill alongside it, through pathless bracken, to its top. A deer fence is just above; turn left alongside it to go through a nearby gate, then left beside the fence. When it turns

walk information

➤ DISTANCE	7.25 miles (11.7km)
➤ MINIMUM TIME	4hrs
➤ ASCENT/GRADIENT	1,300ft (396m) ▲▲▲
➤ LEVEL OF DIFFICULTY	👤👤👤
➤ PATHS	Tracks, one vanished pathless section, 2 stiles
➤ LANDSCAPE	Foothills of Monadhliath, birchwood hollows
➤ SUGGESTED MAPS	OS Explorer 400 Loch Lochy & Glen Roy
➤ START/FINISH	Grid reference: NH 378080
➤ DOG FRIENDLINESS	Can be off lead, unless passing sheep
➤ PARKING	Southern edge of Fort Augustus, signed lane leads off A82 to burial ground
➤ PUBLIC TOILETS	Fort Augustus

downhill, a green path continues ahead, gently uphill through heather. Far ahead and above, pylons crossing the skyline mark the Corrieyairack Pass. The path bends right to join the Corrieyairack track just above.

5 Turn right. The track passes a knoll on the right and this heathery rise marks the highest point of this walk. It then descends in sweeping curves for 1.25 miles (2km). The pass is still technically a road, and it is now a scheduled ancient monument and protected by law. Any person found damaging it will be prosecuted. From here the track climbs gently to rejoin the upward route. At the final bend, a stile offers a short cut through (rather than round) the ancient burial ground.

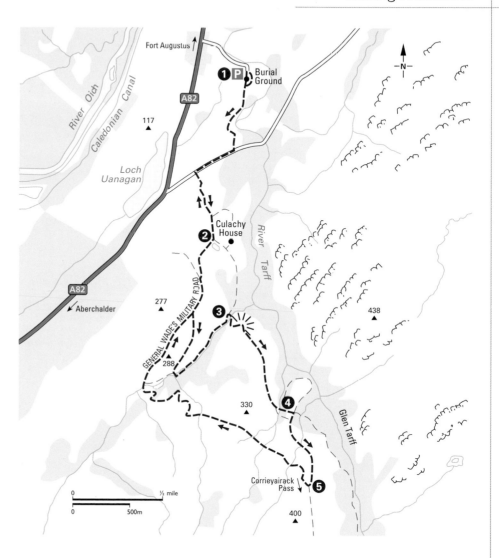

*A rugged waterfall walk into
the hidden hollow where the
MacDonalds hid their stolen cows.*

Into the Lost Valley

*ABOVE: Buachaille Etive Beag
LEFT: The Pass of Glen Coe*

The romantically named Lost Valley is 'Coire Gabhail' in Gaelic, the 'Corrie of Booty'. Here, during the centuries leading up to the famous massacre of 1692, the MacDonalds hid their stolen cattle when the owners came storming in over the Moor of Rannoch with torch and claymore. It seems incredible that even the sure-footed black cattle of the clans could have been persuaded up the slope to Coire Gabhail. The corrie entrance is blocked by two old landslides from the face of Gearr Aonach, the middle hill of Glen Coe's Three Sisters.

Noble Profession of Cattle Thief

The economic system of Highland Scotland, until 1745, was based on the keeping and the stealing of cattle. It was an unsettled and dangerous lifestyle, and its artform was the verse of the bard who celebrated the most ingenious or violent acts of thievery and kept track of blood feuds.

The clan, gathered under its chieftain, was an organisation for protecting its own glen and for stealing from its neighbours. The MacDonalds of Glen Coe were particularly good at it. They raided right across the country, passing the fringes of the Cairngorms to steal from Aberdeenshire and Moray. In 1689, when Campbell of Glen Lyon was a guest in the house of MacIan, chief of Glen Coe, his cold blue eyes may have dwelt on a particular cooking pot. Twice in the previous ten years, MacIan had come raiding into Glen Lyon, dishonoured the women by cutting off their hair and, on the second occasion, stolen that pot from Campbell's own mother.

The Massacre

By the late 1600s, the clan and the claymore were being replaced by a legal system backed by the central government and its army. But because they were so good at cattle thieving, the MacDonalds of Glen Coe continued the practice long after everyone else had, reluctantly, started to move into the modern world of cash. As a result, the government decided to make an example of them.

On a cold February day, a squad of soldiers arrived in the valley. Traditional hospitality meant that even its leader from Glen Lyon, a Campbell and an enemy, was welcomed into the house of MacDonald. Five nights later, at a given signal, the soldiers rose and murdered their hosts. The Glen Coe Massacre was either incompetent or mercifully half-hearted. Of the valley's population of 300, just 40 were killed, with the remainder escaping through the snow to the Lost Valley and other high corries.

RIGHT: Adnach Eagach Ridge, Glen Coe

walk directions

1 From the uphill corner of the car park, a faint path slants down to the old road, which is now a well-used wide path. Head up the valley for about 650yds (594m). With the old road continuing as a green track ahead, your path now bends down to the right. It has been rebuilt, with the bog problem solved by scraping down to the bedrock. The path reaches the gorge where the River Coe runs in a geological dyke of softer rock. Descend here on a steep wooden step ladder, to cross a spectacular footbridge.

2 The ascent out of the gorge is on a bare rock staircase. Above, the path runs through regenerating birch wood, which can be very wet on the legs; sheep and deer have been excluded from the wood with a temporary fence. Emerge from this through a high gate. The path, rebuilt in places, runs uphill for 60yds (55m). Here it bends left; an inconspicuous alternative path continues uphill, and can be used to bypass the narrow path of the main route.

3 The main route contours into the gorge of the Allt Coire Gabhail. It is narrow with steep drops below. Where there is an alternative of rock slabs and a narrow path just below, the slabs are more secure. You will hear waterfalls, then two fine ones come into view ahead. After passing these, continue between boulders to where the main path bends left to cross the stream below a boulder the size of a small house. (A small path runs on up to the right of the stream, but leads nowhere useful.) The river here is wide and fairly shallow. Five or six stepping stones usually allow dry crossing. If the water is above the stones, then it's safer to wade alongside them; if the water is more than knee-deep the crossing should not be attempted.

LEFT: Beech trees in Glen Coe Wood

walk information

➤ **DISTANCE**	2.75 miles (4.4km)
➤ **MINIMUM TIME**	2hrs 15min
➤ **ASCENT/GRADIENT**	1,050ft (320m) ▲▲▲
➤ **LEVEL OF DIFFICULTY**	🚶🚶🚶
➤ **PATHS**	Rugged and stony, stream to wade through
➤ **LANDSCAPE**	Crags and mountains
➤ **SUGGESTED MAPS**	OS Explorer 384 Glen Coe & Glen Etive
➤ **START/FINISH**	Grid reference: NN 168569
➤ **DOG FRIENDLINESS**	Dogs must be reasonably fit and agile
➤ **PARKING**	Lower of two roadside parking places opposite Gearr Aonach (middle one of Three Sisters)
➤ **PUBLIC TOILETS**	Glencoe village

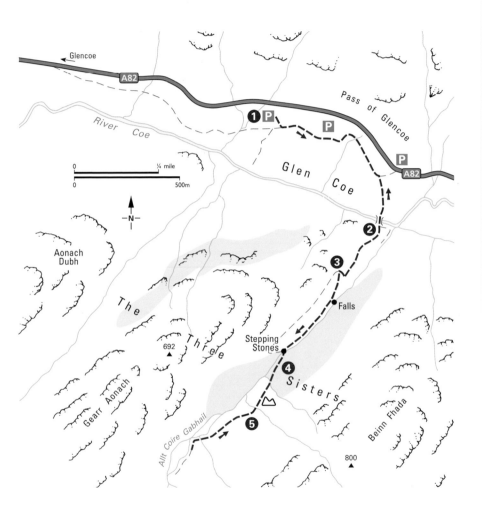

4 A well-built path continues uphill, now with the stream on its right. After 100yds (91m), a lump of rock blocks the way. The path follows a slanting ramp up its right-hand side. It continues uphill, still rebuilt in places, passing above the boulder pile that blocks the valley, the result of two large rockfalls from under Gearr Aonach opposite. At the top of the rockpile the path levels, giving a good view into the Lost Valley.

5 Drop gently to the valley's gravel floor. The stream vanishes into the gravel, to reappear below the boulder pile on the other side. Note where the path arrives at the gravel, as it becomes invisible at that point. Wander up the valley to where the stream vanishes, 0.25 mile (400m) ahead. Anywhere beyond this point is more serious hillwalking than you have done up to now on this walk. Return to the path and follow it back to the start of the walk.

*A deeply wooded riverside
leads from the famous battlefield
to Loch Faskally.*

The Braes o' Killiecrankie

*Ye wouldna been sae swanky o
If ye'd hae seen where I hae seen
On the braes o Killiecrankie o*

The song commemorating the victory of the Battle of Killiecrankie in July 1689 is still sung wherever anyone with an accordion sits down in a pub full of patriotic tourists. In fact, both sides in the battle were Scots. When James II was ousted from England in a bloodless coup in 1688, the Scots Parliament (the Estates) voted to replace him with William of Orange. The Stuarts had neglected and mismanaged Scotland, and had mounted a bloody persecution of the fundamentalist Protestants (Covenanters) of the Southern Uplands.

ABOVE: The Pitlochry Hydro Hotel
RIGHT: Loch Faskally

'Bluidy Clavers'

John Claverhouse, 'Bonnie Dundee', had earned the rather different nickname 'Bluidy Clavers' in those persecutions. He now raised a small army of Highlanders in support of King James. The Estates sent a larger army north under another Highlander, General Hugh Mackay, to sort things out. Dundee, outnumbered two to one, was urged to ambush Mackay in the Pass of Killiecrankie. He refused, on the grounds of chivalry. The path above the river was steep, muddy and wide enough for only two soldiers; a surprise attack on such difficult ground would give his broadsword-wielding Highlanders too great an advantage against Mackay's inexperienced troops. Just one of the Lowlanders was picked off by an Atholl sharpshooter at the Trouper's Den (below today's visitor centre), and the battle actually took place on open ground, to the north of the pass.

Claymore Victorious

Killiecrankie was the last time the claymore conquered the musket in open battle, due to a deficiency in the musket. Some 900 of the 2,500 Highlanders were shot down as they charged, but then the troopers had to stop to fix their bayonets, which plugged into the muzzle of the musket. By this time the Highlanders were upon them, and they broke and fled. The battle had lasted just three minutes. Half of Mackay's army was killed, wounded, captured or drowned in the Garry. One escaped by leaping 18ft (5.5m) across the river: the 'Soldier's Leap'. Dundee died in battle. A month later his army was defeated at Dunkeld, and 25 years later, when the Highlanders next brought their claymores south for the Stuarts, the troupers had learnt to fix a bayonet to the side of a musket where it didn't block the barrel.

ABOVE: A marching tartan bagpipe band closing the Pitlochry Highland Games

walk directions

1 From the back corner of the visitor centre, steps signed 'Soldier's Leap' lead down into the wooded gorge. A footbridge crosses the waterfall of Trouper's Den. At the next junction, turn left ('Soldier's Leap'). Ten steps down, a spur path on the right leads to the viewpoint above the Soldier's Leap.

2 Return to the main path, signed 'Linn of Tummel', which runs down to the River Garry below the railway viaduct. After 1 mile (1.6km), the path reaches a footbridge.

3 Don't cross this footbridge, but continue ahead, signed 'Pitlochry', along the riverside under the tall South Garry road bridge. The path bears left to a footbridge. Cross and turn right, signed 'Pitlochry', back to the main river. The path runs around a huge river pool to a tarred lane; turn right here. The lane leaves the lochside, then passes a track on the right, blocked by a vehicle barrier. Ignore this track; shortly afterwards turn right at a signpost, 'Pitlochry'.

4 Immediately bear left to pass along the right-hand side of Loch Dunmore, following red-top posts. A footbridge crosses the loch, but turn away from it, half right, on to a small path that becomes a dirt track. After 270yds (250m) it reaches a wider track. Turn left, with a white/yellow waymarker. After 220yds (201m) the track starts to climb; here the white/yellow markers indicate a smaller path on the right, which follows the lochside to a point below the A9 road bridge.

5 Cross Loch Faskally on the Clunie footbridge below the road's bridge and turn right, on a quiet road around the loch. In 1 mile (1.6km), at the top of the grass bank on the left, is the Priest Stone. After you pass the Clunie power station, you reach a car park on the left. Here a sign indicates a steep little path down to the Linn of Tummel.

6 Return to the road above for 0.5 mile (800m), to cross a grey suspension bridge on the right. Turn right, downstream, to pass above the Linn. A spur path back right returns to the falls at a lower level, but the main path continues along the riverside (signed 'Killiecrankie'). It bends left and goes down wooden steps to the Garry, then continues upstream and under the high road bridge. Take the side-path up on to the bridge for the view of the river, then return to follow the descending path signed 'Pitlochry via Faskally'. This runs down to the bridge, Point 3. Return upstream to the start.

walk information

➤ **DISTANCE**	8.75 miles (14.1km)
➤ **MINIMUM TIME**	4hrs
➤ **ASCENT/GRADIENT**	492ft (150m) ▲ ▲▲
➤ **LEVEL OF DIFFICULTY**	✝✝✝
➤ **PATHS**	Wide riverside paths, minor road, no stiles
➤ **LANDSCAPE**	Oakwoods on banks of two rivers
➤ **SUGGESTED MAPS**	OS Explorer 386 Pitlochry & Loch Tummel
➤ **START/FINISH**	Grid reference: NN 917626
➤ **DOG FRIENDLINESS**	Off lead on riverside paths
➤ **PARKING**	Killiecrankie visitor centre
➤ **PUBLIC TOILETS**	At start

Looking along Loch Awe from Cruachan Reservoir, Britain's biggest energy storage system.

The Hill with the Hole

The Cruachan Reservoir collects rainfall from a fairly small catchment, 9 square miles (23sq km) bounded by the rocky ridge of Ben Cruachan. Even with Cruachan's 116in (2,945mm) of rain a year, only 4 megawatts of power are generated, not enough to supply Oban, to the west.

ABOVE: Sunset over Kilchurn Castle
LEFT: Kilchurn Castle, Loch Awe

The Big Battery

Cruachan is more than just a rather small power station; it's a rechargeable storage system for electrical energy, a very big electric battery. The demand for electric power varies from day to day, and even from minute to minute. There's the surge, for example during the advertising break in your favourite soap as a million kettles get switched on at once. Coal and oil power stations can be stoked up or cooled off, but only quite gradually. Nuclear stations run at the same rate day and night. And the greenest energy sources, wind and wave generators, give power according to the weather. So there has to be a way of taking electricity out of the National Grid when there's too much, and putting it back when it's most needed.

Cruachan Power

Fortunately, an electric generator running backwards becomes a motor, and a turbine turns into a pump. At 'white-meter' (off-peak) times of day, water is pumped from Loch Awe up to Cruachan Reservoir, 1,000ft (305m) above. And at 7:15 on a weekday evening, it flows back down again.

The stored energy in the battery of your car is sufficient to keep it running for about half a minute, but that's enough to start it in the morning and run the CD deck when the engine's off. Full to the brim, Cruachan Reservoir, with the capacity of about half a billion car batteries, in theory holds enough potential energy to supply the UK's peak demand for 10 minutes. In fact the water can't be drawn down that fast, but at full flow Cruachan could supply 400 megawatts, enough for most of Glasgow. Time your arrival for 7:15pm, and you could see the reservoir sinking at an inch (2.5cm) per minute. The same amount of water will be flowing out into Loch Awe, just beside the visitor centre. The whole process – pumping up and then retrieving the potential energy – is not much more than 50 per cent efficient. The waste heat ends up in Loch Awe, where it benefits the fish farm opposite the visitor centre.

The Secret Source

The Cruachan powerhouse makes a fairly small impact on the outer world. Around 12 miles (19km) of pipes bring water into the reservoir, and the outgoing or incoming electricity loops across the hill on high pylons. The 1,030ft (315m) dam is only visible once you reach the corrie; the power station itself is actually buried deep in the heart of the mountain.

walk directions

1 Two paths run up on either side of the Falls of Cruachan. Both are initially rough and steep through woodland. The western one starts at a tarred lane opposite the entrance to the power station proper (not the visitor centre, slightly further to the west). This diminishes to a track, which becomes rough and crosses the railway as a level crossing. A path continues uphill in steep zig-zags through birch, rowan and oak. There are various points to stop and admire Loch Awe, which disappears glittering in the distance. White speckled stones in the path are Cruachan granite. The path continues on steeply to the top of the wood.

2 Here a high ladder stile crosses a deer fence. With the stream on your right, continue uphill on the small path to a track below the Cruachan dam. Turn left, up to the base of the dam, which measures 1,030ft (315m) wide and 150ft (46m) high. Because it's tucked back into the corrie, it can't be seen from below, but it is clearly visible from the top of Dun na Cuaiche, 12 miles (19.3km) away. The hollows between the 13 huge buttresses send back a fine echo. Steps on the left lead up below the base of the dam, then iron steps take you on to the dam's top.

3 From here you can look across the reservoir and up to a skyline that's slightly jagged at the back left corner, where Ben Cruachan's ridge

sharpens to a rocky edge. In the other direction, your tough ascent is rewarded by a long view across Lorn. Turn right to the dam end, where a track leads down right to a junction, then right for 50yds (46m).

4 At this point you could stay on the track to cross the concrete bridge just ahead, leading to the top of the path used for coming up. Otherwise there is a clear path as you go down to the left of the stream, to reach a high, steep ladder stile. (There's a useful dog flap in the deer fence alongside.) Below this there is a clear path that descends grassy slopes and gives a good view of some of the Falls of Cruachan. Inside the wood, the path becomes steep and rough for the rest of the way down. Just above the railway, it turns left, then passes under the line by a low tunnel beside Falls of Cruachan Station, to the A85.

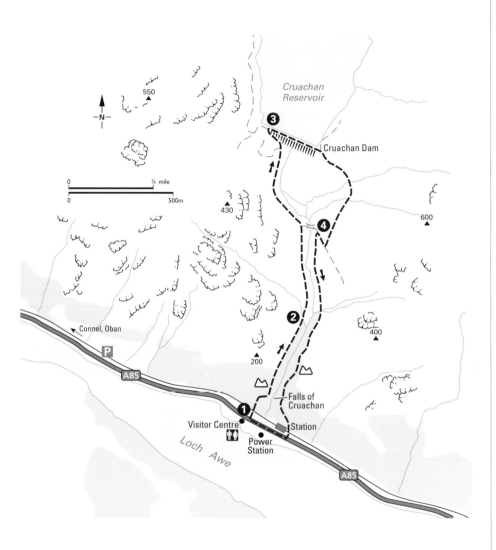

walk information

➤ **DISTANCE**	2 miles (3.2km)
➤ **MINIMUM TIME**	1hr 45min
➤ **ASCENT/GRADIENT**	1,200ft (366m) ▲▲▲
➤ **LEVEL OF DIFFICULTY**	🚶🚶🚶
➤ **PATHS**	Steep, rugged paths, 2 ladder stiles
➤ **LANDSCAPE**	Wooded slopes and high corrie
➤ **SUGGESTED MAPS**	OS Explorer 377 Loch Etive & Glen Orchy
➤ **START/FINISH**	Grid reference: NN 078268
➤ **DOG FRIENDLINESS**	Good, but high and steep ladder stiles to negotiate
➤ **PARKING**	Two pull-ins on north side of A85, below railway station. Also lay-by 0.5 mile (800m) west. Not visitor centre car park
➤ **PUBLIC TOILETS**	Cruachan Visitor Centre

Dun na Cuaiche offers a fine view of Inveraray, Campbell capital of Argyll.

Climbing to the Castle of Cups

Inveraray, on the shores of Loch Fyne, is the seat of the Duke of Argyll, chieftain of Clan Campbell. It is a fine example of town planning, created by the 3rd Duke of Argyll in the 1740s. The little town is stylish, with a wide main street of white-painted houses running up to the classical kirk (church). Thus it became, in the eyes of Campbells anyway, the capital of the southern Highlands.

ABOVE: Inveraray and Loch Fyne
RIGHT: Inveraray Castle was built in 1743 for the 3rd Duke of Argyll

The Campbells Have Come

Until about 1600, the main power in the Highlands was MacDonald, Lord of the Isles. The Duke of Argyll aimed to take his place – by the normal methods of intrigue and armed attack on neighbouring clans, but also by collaboration with the legal government in Edinburgh and the King in London. Clan Campbell would hit you with fire and the sword, but also with a writ from the Privy Council. As a result they became the most powerful and the most universally disliked of all the clans.

In 1691, King William demanded an oath of loyalty from the rebellious Highland chieftains. MacIan of the Glen Coe MacDonalds was required to sign his oath in Inveraray. He hesitated over this visit to the capital of his hated rivals, and eventually arrived two days after the deadline. His delay was made the pretext for the Campbell-led Massacre of Glen Coe. When a Campbell was murdered in Appin 60 years later, the suspect, James Stewart of the Glens, was tried at Inveraray before a jury of Campbells, with Argyll himself as judge. The hanging of Stewart, who was almost certainly innocent, is still resented in the MacDonald country.

Argyll Rebuilds

With the breaking of the clan system in 1745, Argyll felt confident enough to pull down his fortified castle and rebuild in a grand residential style that suited a wealthy landowner who no longer needed to resort to violence to keep control over his lands.

The present building, greatly admired by Sir Walter Scott, is described as a country house in the style of a castle. Its grey stone, quarried from just above the town, is sombre, but tones well with the muted green and blue of the Campbell tartan. To go with his new castle, Argyll decided he needed a new town. Some say that old Inveraray was simply too close to the castle. But in its present position, curved around its bay, it's a magnificent and early example of a modern, planned town. It is dominated by the Court House where James of the Glens stood his trial, and by the white arches of the Argyll Hotel. One of these arches is a passageway for the A819.

The Duke of Argyll completed his ambitious rebuilding scheme with avenues and bridges; one of the bridges forms an elegant entry to the town on the A83. This walk crosses the Garden Bridge, designed by John Adam (1721–92) of the Scottish family of architects. The whole layout of castle and town is seen from the summit of Dun na Cuaiche (Castle of Cups).

walk directions

1 Follow the seafront past the Argyll Hotel and bear left towards Inveraray Castle. At the first junction, turn right past a football pitch with a standing stone. After the coach park on the left and the end wall of the castle on the right, the estate road on the left is signed 'Dun na Cuaiche Woodland Walks'. It passes a memorial to clansmen who were killed for religious reasons in 1685. Cross the stone-arched Garden Bridge to a junction.

2 Half-right now is the uphill path with coloured waymarkers that will be the return leg of the walk. During the coming summers this may be affected by timber lorries, in which case there will be a notice closing this path. If you should see such a notice, it is fine to continue with the route described below up to Dun na Cuaiche, Point 4, before returning by the way you came up, via Point 3. Turn right on a riverside track and follow it to a picnic table with a view back to the castle. A rough track runs up left, but turn off instead on to a small path just to the right of this, beside a stone gatepost. It climbs quite steeply through an area where attempts have failed to eradicate rhododendron.

3 At a green track above, turn right, slightly uphill, for 100yds (91m) to a turning circle. Turn left up a muddy path under trees. This improves, bending left and slanting uphill across a stream. The path continues directly uphill under birch trees, with a stream nearby on its left through woods. As the slope eases, the path crosses a grassy clearing to meet a wider one. Turn left, in zig-zags, to reach the summit of Dun na Cuaiche. The tower offers outstanding views.

walk information

➤ **DISTANCE**	4 miles (6.4km)
➤ **MINIMUM TIME**	2hrs 15min
➤ **ASCENT/GRADIENT**	900ft (274m) ▲▲▲
➤ **LEVEL OF DIFFICULTY**	🚶🚶🚶
➤ **PATHS**	Clear, mostly waymarked paths, no stiles
➤ **LANDSCAPE**	Steep, wooded hill, some rocky outcrops
➤ **SUGGESTED MAPS**	OS Explorer 363 Cowal East
➤ **START/FINISH**	Grid reference: NN 096085
➤ **DOG FRIENDLINESS**	Must be under control, not necessarily on lead
➤ **PARKING**	Pay-and-display, Inveraray Pier
➤ **PUBLIC TOILETS**	Inveraray Pier and Castle

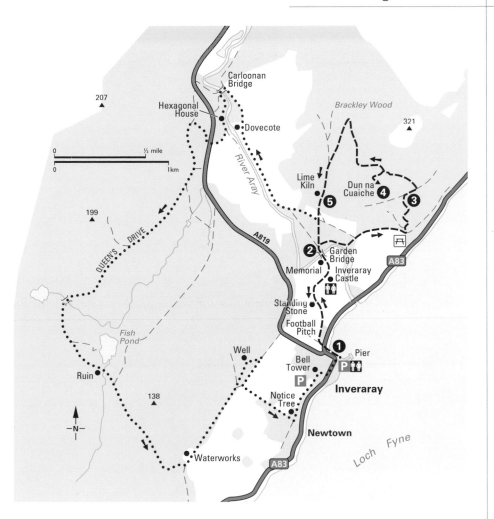

4 Return down the path to the clearing, but this time keep ahead. The path, rather muddy, bends left then enters the plantation and becomes a clear track. It passes between two dry-stone pillars where a wall crosses, turns back sharp left, and passes between two more pillars lower down the same wall. Continue down the track, ignoring side-tracks on the left, to a lime kiln on the right.

5 Past the lime kiln, a gate leads into a field. Fork right off the track, re-crossing it below to a gate beyond. This leads into a wood. The path runs down to the track junction before the Garden Bridge (Point 2). Return along the castle driveway to Inveraray.

Extending the Walk

From Point 5, you could take the track on the right, to head upstream to the right of River Aray, past a white dovecote and through Carloonan farm. Cross Carloonan Bridge and head back downstream on a track that bends right to the A819. Turn right on an old road opposite to a path on the left. At a T-junction, turn left over a stream. With the track about to rejoin the A819, turn right and keep right at the next fork to follow Queen's Drive through Coillebhraghad Wood. It passes to the right of a large fishpond. In 440yds (402m) keep ahead on a smaller track, down a pretty wooded glen to a waterworks. Turn left along the wooded footpath. With a metal turnpike gate on the right, fork up left to visit the ornamental well. Return to the turnpike gate, which leads out towards Newtown. At the notice tree, turn left to Inveraray.

*On this easy town trail, discover an
ancient university, which observes
some very strange traditions.*

Academic Traditions at St Andrews

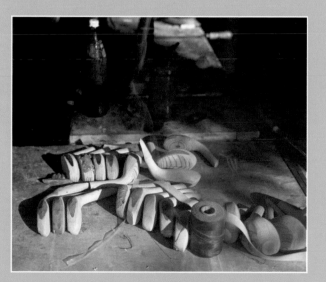

S t Andrews is famous for two things –
as the home of golf and of an ancient
university. A small town on the Fife
coast, it has an atmosphere all its own and feels
quite unlike any other town in Scotland.

*ABOVE: Golf clubs in the making
in a St Andrews shop
LEFT: Ruins of the Cathedral
of St Andrews*

Reasons for Raisins

The university was established in 1410 and is the oldest in Scotland, and third oldest in Britain – after Oxford and Cambridge. The first faculties established here were theology, canon law, civil law, medicine and arts, with theology being of particular importance. In medieval times students could enter the university as young as 13, and a system of seniority soon arose among the student body. New students were known as bejaunus, from the French 'bec-jaune' or fledgling, and were initiated into the fraternity on Raisin Monday, when they were expected to produce a pound of raisins in return for a cheeky receipt. The tradition persists today, with bejants, as they are now known (females are bejantines), being taken under the wings of older students who become their 'academic parents'. On Raisin Sunday, in November, academic 'fathers' take their charges out to get thoroughly drunk. On the next day, Raisin Monday, the 'mothers' put them in fancy dress before they and their hangovers congregate in St Salvator's quad for a flour and egg fight.

Elizabeth Garrett, the first woman in Britain to qualify as a doctor, was allowed to matriculate at St Andrews in 1862 but was then rejected after the Senate declared her enrolment illegal. Following this the university made efforts to encourage the education of women, who were eventually allowed full membership of the university in 1892. In 1866 Elizabeth Garrett established a dispensary for women in London, which later became the famous Elizabeth Garrett Anderson Hospital.

Treasured Traditions

The university is proud of its traditions and, as you walk around the streets today, you might well spot students wearing their distinctive scarlet gowns. These were introduced after 1640 and some say they were brightly coloured so that students could be spotted when entering the local brothels. They are made of a woolly fabric with a velvet yoke. First-year students wear them over both shoulders, gradually casting them off each year, until in their fourth and final year the gowns hang down, almost dragging behind them.

Other university traditions include a Sunday walk along the pier after church, which continued until the pier was closed for repair, and a mass dawn swim in the sea on May morning (1 May). Given the icy nature of the waters, this is not an activity to be attempted by the faint-hearted.

walk information

➤ **DISTANCE**	4.5 miles (7.2km)
➤ **MINIMUM TIME**	2hrs
➤ **ASCENT/GRADIENT**	33ft (10m) ▲▲▲
➤ **LEVEL OF DIFFICULTY**	𐐒𐐒𐐒𐐒
➤ **PATHS**	Ancient streets and golden sands
➤ **LANDSCAPE**	Historic university town and windy seascapes
➤ **SUGGESTED MAPS**	OS Explorer 371 St Andrews & East Fife
➤ **START/FINISH**	Grid reference: NO 506170
➤ **DOG FRIENDLINESS**	Dogs not permitted on beach
➤ **PARKING**	Free parking along The Scores, otherwise several car parks
➤ **PUBLIC TOILETS**	Several close to beach

walk directions

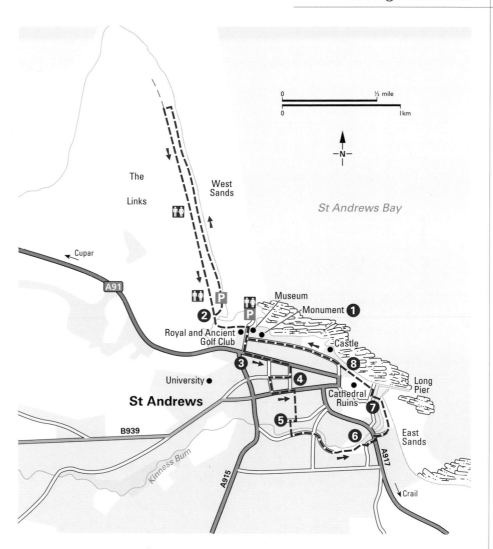

1 With the Martyrs Monument on The Scores in front of you, walk left past the bandstand. At the road turn right, walk to the British Golf Museum, then turn left. Pass the clubhouse of the Royal and Ancient Golf Club on your left, then bear right at the burn to reach the beach.

2 Your route now takes you along the West Sands. Walk as far as you choose, then either retrace your steps along the beach or take one of the paths through the dunes to join the tarmac road. Walk back to the Golf Museum, then turn right and walk to the main road.

3 Turn left along the road and walk to St Salvator's College. Take a peek through the archway at the serene quadrangle – and look at the initials PH in the cobbles outside. They commemorate Patrick Hamilton, who was martyred here in 1528 – they say students who tread on the site will fail their exams. Now cross over and walk to the end of College Street.

4 Turn right and walk along Market Street. At the corner turn left along Bell Street, then left again on South Street. Opposite Holy Trinity Church, turn right down Queens Gardens to reach Queens Terrace.

5 Turn right then immediately left down steeply sloping Dempster Terrace. At the end cross the burn, turn left and walk to the main road. Cross over and walk along Glebe Road. At the park, take the path that bears left, walk past the play area and up to Woodburn Terrace.

6 Turn left to join St Mary Street and cross over the main road to follow Woodburn Place down towards the beach. Just before the slipway, turn left along a tarmac path. Cross over the footbridge and join the road.

7 Bear right for a few paces, then ascend the steps on the left. These bring you up to the remains of a church and on to the famous ruined cathedral. A gate in the wall on the left gives access to the site.

8 Your route then follows the beachfront past the ancient castle on the right. A former palace/fortress, it was at the forefront of the Reformation – John Knox preached here. Pass the Castle Visitor Centre, then continue along The Scores to return to the car park at the start.

PAGE 60: Inside the cathedral ruins
BELOW: St Andrews is sited alongside long sandy beaches

A short walk back in time to the stone shrines and monuments in the valley of the ghosts.

The Neolithic Monuments of Kilmartin Glen

ABOVE: *Temple Wood Standing Stones, Kilmartin*

K ilmartin Glen with its lush alluvial plains, easy landfalls on the coast near Crinan and an abundant supply of water has attracted human settlers since the earliest times. In around 5000 BC, nomadic hunter-gatherers frequented this area but left little evidence of their presence other than piles of bones and shells in caves.

Early Settlers

The arrival of small groups of neolithic people from around 3000 BC provided the first lasting signs of habitation. These early settlers, farmers and skilled weavers and potters, cleared the ground for grazing and erected the first stone shrines and circles. What they were for is not certain, but they were probably an early form of astronomical calendar for determining when to plant and harvest crops or to move cattle. They were probably also part of religious rituals closely related to the seasons and survival. Around Kilmartin Glen 25 different sites of standing stones have been found. Some are simple arrangements, others single stones, while in Temple Wood the monument consists of two stone circles.

Great Monuments

Later, Bronze Age people were responsible for the monuments that can still be seen in the prehistoric linear cemetery, built over the course of 1,000 years, that runs for a mile (1.6km) down the glen. Each of the huge stone-lined burial chambers is slightly different in design and construction.

The Glebe Cairn, which looks like a pile of boulders with a cap stone, is situated near the church and is typical of the burial cairns of the period 1700–1500 BC. At the centre of this cairn were two stone cists for the burials and these contained pottery and a necklace of jet beads. The next tomb south from here, known as the North Tomb, has been rebuilt over a modern shelter that allows access through a hatch and contains a large slab carved with pictures of axe heads and cupmarks. The last cairn in this direction, the South Cairn is the earliest and was originally a chambered tomb dating from 4000 BC.

In the Iron Age, warring tribes ringed the glen with hill-forts and it was on one of these, at Dunadd, that the Scotti tribe from Ireland founded their capital in the 6th century AD. St Columba came to Kilmartin in the same century and established the first Christian church here.

Within Kilmartin parish church can be found relics from a later age. The ornately carved Kilmartin Cross depicts one of the most moving images of Christ to have survived from the early Scottish Christian Church and the churchyard has one of the finest collections of ornately carved medieval gravestones in Scotland.

RIGHT: Sheep graze in a field beside the Temple Wood Standing Stones

walk information

➤ **DISTANCE**	3.5 miles (5.7km)
➤ **MINIMUM TIME**	3hrs
➤ **ASCENT/GRADIENT**	Negligible ▲▲▲
➤ **LEVEL OF DIFFICULTY**	🏃🏃🏃
➤ **PATHS**	Boggy fields, old coach road and country lanes, 3 stiles
➤ **LANDSCAPE**	Pasture, hills, woodland
➤ **SUGGESTED MAPS**	OS Explorer 358 Lochgilphead & Knapdale North
➤ **START/FINISH**	Grid reference: NR 835988
➤ **DOG FRIENDLINESS**	Dogs fine on route
➤ **PARKING**	Car park outside Kilmartin church
➤ **PUBLIC TOILETS**	Kilmartin House

walk directions

1 From the car park visit Kilmartin church to marvel at the stones and see the Kilmartin Cross. Leave the church, turn left and walk along the road past Kilmartin House, exit the village and head downhill towards a garage on the left. Just before the garage turn left, go through a kissing gate and head across the field to the Glebe Cairn.

2 From the cairn head half right, across the field to cross a stile. In wet weather this can be very boggy so stout footwear is advisable. Cross the stream by a bridge. Go through a gate and turn left on to the old coach road. Follow this to the next cairn. Go left over a stile and follow the path to visit the cairn.

3 Return to the road and turn left, continuing to the next cairn. After exploring this, follow the coach road to Kilmartin school, where the route becomes a metalled road.

Go through a crossroads, past Nether Largie farm and, ignoring the cairn on the left, continue a short distance to Temple Wood ahead on the right.

4 Go through a gate on the right into Temple Wood, then return by the same route. Turn right on to the road and continue until you reach a T-junction. Turn left and walk along this road until you come to a sign on the right for Ri Cruin Cairn. Cross the wall via a stile and proceed along the well-defined path to see the ancient monument.

5 Return by the same route and turn right on to the road. Follow it to a T-junction then turn left and keep straight ahead until you reach the car park at Lady Glassary Wood. Opposite this take a path to the left signposted to Temple Wood. Cross a bridge, go through a gate and head towards the standing stones.

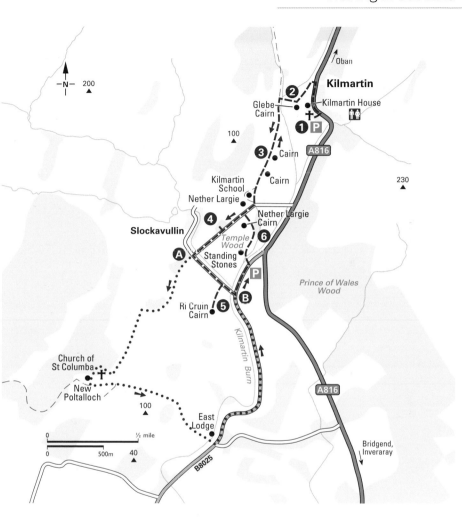

6 Turn right and walk across the field away from the stones towards a wood. Go through a gate and follow the fenced path to Nether Largie Cairn. From here continue along the fenced path, go through another gate and turn right on to the road. Continue past Nether Largie farm and Kilmartin school and then retrace your steps back to reach Kilmartin church and the car park.

ABOVE: A view over the surrounding countryside at Kilmartin

Extending the Walk

Extend the walk from Point A by following a dilapidated estate track towards the Church of St Columba and New Poltalloch. The ruins of this enourmous neo-Jacobean mansion can be seen to good effect from the estate track on the other side. Continue through to East Lodge, where you should turn left along the road to meet up with the main route again at Point B.

Discover the truth about the ultimate Scottish hero on this town trail.

Stirling's Braveheart, William Wallace

To many Scots he is the ultimate hero, a charismatic patriot who died fighting for his country's freedom. To others he is less exalted – an outlaw and murderer. Discovering the truth about William Wallace is not easy, as few contemporary accounts exist, although we can be reasonably assured that he didn't look like Mel Gibson or paint his face with woad.

ABOVE: In the courtyard of Stirling Castle
LEFT: Looking from the ramparts of Stirling Castle towards the Wallace Monument

Wallace's heroic status is immediately obvious on your arrival in Stirling, which is dominated by the enormous monument erected in his memory. He was born at Ellerslie near Kilmarnock early in the 1270s and little is known of his early life. He might have remained unknown were it not for the fact that in 1286 the Scottish King, Alexander III, was found dead on the sands at Kinghorn, Fife. His only direct heir was Margaret of Norway – and many powerful Scots did not want a woman on the throne. When Margaret died on her way to Scotland, the succession was plunged into further confusion. The only likely contestants were John Balliol and Robert Bruce. Edward I was asked to advise, chose Balliol, and then exerted his authority by demanding revenues from Scotland. Balliol later infuriated Edward by signing a treaty with England's enemy, France, and Edward retaliated by sacking Berwick in 1296, slaughtering thousands. The Scots began to resist, Balliol was deposed as king, and the Wars of Independence began.

Wallace Wages War

Wallace joined the struggle. In 1297 he killed the English Sheriff of Lanark and led a number of attacks on English forces. Later that year he won the battle that was to make his reputation, defeating Edward's army at Stirling Bridge. Wallace's forces killed thousands of English and Welsh troops, driving the wounded into the marshes to drown. Wallace now had considerable power. Faced with the possibility of food shortages in Scotland, he ordered an invasion of northern England to plunder food. Many villagers were murdered, churches were burned and more than 700 villages destroyed.

In 1298 Wallace was made Guardian of Scotland, but was defeated by Edward I later that year at the Battle of Falkirk. He resigned the Guardianship and travelled to Rome to enlist support from the Pope for the restoration of Balliol as king. Back in Scotland, he continually refused to accept Edward as King of Scotland and was eventually captured and taken prisoner in 1305 (some say he was betrayed by Scots). He was executed at Smithfield in London (the torture of being hung, drawn and quartered was invented for him) and immediately became a martyr for Scottish independence.

ABOVE: The statue of Robert the Bruce on the esplanade, Stirling Castle
LEFT: Looking towards the Church of the Holy Rude

walk directions

1 From the tourist information centre on Dumbarton Road, cross the road and turn left. Walk past the statue of Robert Burns then, just before the Albert Halls, turn right and walk back on yourself. Just past the statue of Rob Roy, turn left and take the path along the Back Wall.

2 Almost immediately (20yds/18m) turn right up the flight of steps that takes you on to the Upper Back Wall. It's a steady climb now, past the Church of the Holy Rude, where James VI was crowned in 1567 and past Ladies' Rock – where ladies of the castle sat to watch tournaments.

3 Continue following the path uphill to reach Stirling Castle. Cross the car park to take the path running downhill just to the side of the visitor centre, so that the castle is on your left. At the cemetery, turn right along the footpath signposted to Moto Hill. Continue up steps and across the cemetery to the gap in the wall.

4 Follow the track downhill on to Gowan Hill. There are several branching tracks but you continue on the main path – heading for the cannons on the hill ahead. At a junction turn right down a track signposted to Lower Bridge Street. Turn on to a grassy slope to the right to see the Beheading Stone. Retrace your steps to the wide track and then follow it to reach the road.

5 Turn right along Lower Bridge Street, then fork right into Upper Bridge Street. Continue ahead, then 50yds (46m) beyond Settle Inn, turn right up a cobbled lane, it looks a bit like the access to a house. Follow it uphill, then go left at the top. Eventually you'll pass the Castle Esplanade, followed by Argyll's Lodging, and will reach a junction.

6 Turn left, passing Hermann's Restaurant and the Mercat Cross. Turn right at the bottom down Bow Street, then left along Baker Street. When you reach Friars Street (which is pedestrianised), turn left and walk down to the end.

7 Turn right now, then first left to reach the station. Turn left, then right over the bridge, then bear left in front of new development to reach the

walk information

➤ **DISTANCE**	5 miles (8km)
➤ **MINIMUM TIME**	2hrs 30 min
➤ **ASCENT/GRADIENT**	279ft (85m) ▲▲▲
➤ **LEVEL OF DIFFICULTY**	👥👥👥
➤ **PATHS**	Ancient city streets and some rough tracks
➤ **LANDSCAPE**	Bustling little city topped with magnificent castle
➤ **SUGGESTED MAPS**	OS Explorer 366 Stirling & Ochil Hills West
➤ **START/FINISH**	Grid reference: NS 795933
➤ **DOG FRIENDLINESS**	Mostly on lead, not good for those that dislike crowds
➤ **PARKING**	On streets near TIC or in multi-storey car parks
➤ **PUBLIC TOILETS**	At visitor centre by the castle

riverside. Maintain direction and join Abbey Road. Bear left at the end, go right over the footbridge and continue along South Street, turning right at the end to visit the remains of Cambuskenneth Abbey.

8 Retrace your steps back to the station. Turn right, then left, then right again at the Thistle Shopping Centre. Go along Port Street, then turn right along Dumbarton Road to return to the start.

Extending the Walk

You can add a loop to this walk by crossing Old Stirling Bridge and walking up the road to the foot of the Wallace Monument. After you've scaled the heights to the statue, come back to the road and turn left, then right, over the railway to Cambuskenneth Abbey, where you can pick up the main route at Point 8.

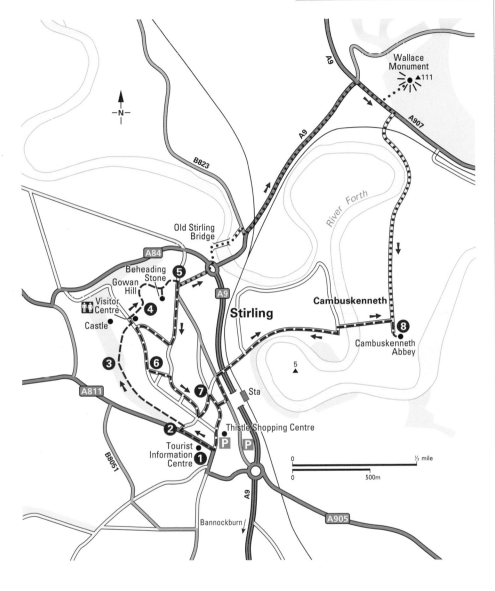

LEFT: *The Wallace Monument was erected in 1869*

73

An easy walk that ends on the cobbled streets of an historic town, where a prosperous trading history is reflected in the buildings.

A Leisurely Circuit of Culross

Walking through Culross is a bit like stepping on to a film set. With its cobbled streets and immaculately preserved buildings, it gives you the impression that you've stepped back in time. The pretty houses, with their red pantiled roofs and crow-stepped gables, give the place a Flemish look, a typical feature of Scottish architecture of this period. Yet despite its neatly manicured appearance, Culross owes its origins to coal mining.

ABOVE: Detail of the ceiling in the study of Culross Palace
RIGHT: Blair Castle set among trees

Monks and Miners

The mining industry was started in the 13th century by the Cistercian monks of Culross Abbey, and a flourishing trade soon developed. Coal production allowed a salt-panning industry to grow up, with fires from inferior quality coal being used to evaporate sea water. By the 16th century Culross was one of the largest ports in Scotland, exporting both coal and salt to the Low Countries and the Baltic. On their return journeys they carried red pantiles as ballast – which were used to give the town's roofs their distinctive appearance. There are reminders of these days throughout the town. The area known as the Sandhaven, for instance, which you pass at the end of this walk, was once the harbour. As you pass it, take a look at the Tron, where officials would weigh export cargoes to assess their tax — you can still see the stone platform that supported the weighing beam.

Culross Palace

Trade brought prosperity to the town, as you can see from the many substantial buildings that dot the streets. Most striking of all is Culross Palace, a beautiful ochre-coloured town house. It was built in 1597 by Sir George Bruce, the local bigwig who owned both the mines and the salt pans – the pine-panelled walls, decorative paintings and period furniture reflect the lifestyle of a rich merchant of the period. If you go on a tour, look out for the Flemish-style paintings on the wooden ceiling in the Painted Chamber.

Eventually the industries in Culross died out and the village went to sleep, its period features preserved like those of an insect trapped in amber. However, in 1923 the palace was bought by the National Trust for Scotland, which then went on to purchase more properties in the village.

As you near the end of this walk, make time to explore. Walking down the hill you'll pass The House with the Evil Eyes – so named because of the shape of its windows – then the church and the remains of Culross Abbey, before coming into the centre of the village. Look for the street known as The Haggs or Stinking Wynd. If you look carefully you'll see that the centre is higher than the edges. This was 'the crown o' the causie', the place where the local toffs walked. The unfortunate hoi polloi had to walk in the gutters – which would have been swimming with – well, you can imagine.

RIGHT: The exterior of Culross Palace

walk information

➤ DISTANCE	3.5 miles (5.7km)
➤ MINIMUM TIME	1hr 30min
➤ ASCENT/GRADIENT	180ft (55m)
➤ LEVEL OF DIFFICULTY	
➤ PATHS	Generally firm paths, some muddy woodland tracks
➤ LANDSCAPE	Ancient town, fields and woodland
➤ SUGGESTED MAPS	OS Explorer 367 Dunfermline & Kirkcaldy
➤ START/FINISH	Grid reference: NS 983859
➤ DOG FRIENDLINESS	Can run free on woodland tracks
➤ PARKING	Culross West car park
➤ PUBLIC TOILETS	By car park in Culross

walk directions

1 From the car park, take steps up to a tarmac path alongside the railway and turn right. Just beyond a reed bed to the right, turn right down steps and follow the path to the road. Cross over to the entrance to Blair Castle, now a convalescent home for miners.

2 Walk up the tarmac drive, which is lined with magnificent rhododendron bushes. Walk ahead until you can see Blair Castle on the left. Before you reach it, take the right-hand turning in the trees and follow it as it bears to the right. Continue until you reach Blair Mains farmhouse, which you'll find on the left.

3 Continue following the track, with fields on either side. Walk ahead until you reach the trees and continue following this track until you reach a metal gate on the left-hand side, just beyond a line of pylons. Look carefully and you should spot a wooden fence post on the right-hand side, with the words 'West Kirk' and 'grave' painted on it in faint white. Take the narrow right-hand path immediately before it, which runs through the trees.

4 Follow this path to go through a kissing gate and continue walking ahead, with trees on your left and fields on your right. Go through another kissing gate, and continue in the same direction. When you reach a crossing of paths, continue ahead along the track and walk under a line of pylons. You will soon pass the remains of a church on the left-hand side.

5 Continue ahead, past the old cemetery, and walk in the same direction until the track joins a tarmac road. Walk in the same direction until you reach a junction. Turn right here and head downhill – watch out for traffic now as the road can be busy. You will soon reach Culross Abbey on the left-hand side.

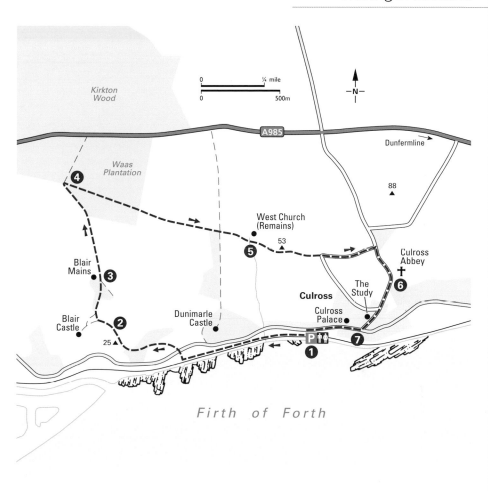

6 It's worth stopping at this point to visit the abbey. You can then continue to walk on downhill, down Tanhouse Brae, and will soon reach the Mercat ('old Market') Cross, with The Study on the right-hand side. Continue walking in the same direction, down Back Causeway, until you reach the main road.

7 Turn right, walk past the tourist information centre, past the Tron (the old burgh weighing machine), then past the large ochre-coloured building on the right, which is Culross Palace. To reach the starting point, continue walking in the same direction – the car park is on the left-hand side, just past the children's play area.

A stroll along Scotland's old canal system to see a strikingly modern 21st-century wheel.

Reinventing the Wheel at Falkirk

The words 'new' and 'unique' are rather overused these days. They seem to be applied to everything from shades of lipstick to formulations of engine oil. But this walk gives you the chance to see something that fully deserves the epithet. The Falkirk Wheel, which opened in the spring of 2002, is the world's first rotating boat lift. It was designed in order to reconnect the Forth and Clyde and Union canals, which stretch across the central belt of Scotland, and so restore a centuries-old link between Glasgow and Edinburgh.

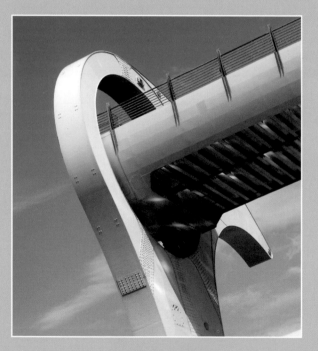

ABOVE AND OVERLEAF: *Details of the Falkirk Wheel*
RIGHT: *The Falkirk Wheel opened in 2002*

Cruising the Canals

The Forth and Clyde Canal, which ran from Grangemouth to Glasgow, was completed in 1790 and made a great difference to the Scottish economy. It opened up a lucrative trading route to America – raw materials could now easily be transported east, while finished products could be shipped west. It also meant that coal extracted from the mines in Lanarkshire could be sent into the newly industrialised areas of Glasgow. The canal was so successful that merchants in Edinburgh soon felt that they were missing out on trade. A plan was devised for another waterway, running from Edinburgh to Falkirk. Work on the Union Canal began in 1818 and a flight of locks was constructed to link it to the Forth and Clyde Canal.

Rise and Fall

The canals were used to transport not only goods but also people. Many preferred to travel by barge than by stage coach, as they were far less bumpy and decidedly warmer. Night boats even had dining rooms and gaming tables. By 1835 more than 127,000 people were travelling on the canal each year. However, shortly afterwards the canal craze began to give way to yet another new innovation – the railways. Train travel, which gained in popularity from the middle of the 19th century, offered cheaper and faster transport, leading to the decline of the canal network. They clung to life until the 1960s, when they were broken up by the expanding network of roads. However, the canals have now been recognised as an important part of Scotland's industrial heritage and are being restored. The Falkirk Wheel was built to replace the original flight of locks, which had been removed in the 1930s, and it's as much a work of art as a feat of engineering. The Wheel lifts boats from one canal to another and is the only rotating boat lift in the world. Made of sharply glinting steel, it's 115ft (35m) high and looks rather like a set of spanners that have fallen from a giant's tool kit. It can carry eight boats at a time and lift loads of 600 tonnes.

An incongruous sight against the gentle tangle of vegetation beside the canal, the Wheel seems to have re-energised the waterways, drawing people to it like a monumental magnet.

walk information	
➤ DISTANCE	2 miles (3.2km); 4 miles (6.4km) with monument
➤ MINIMUM TIME	1hr
➤ ASCENT/GRADIENT	197ft (60m) ▲▲▲
➤ LEVEL OF DIFFICULTY	🚶🚶🚶
➤ PATHS	Canal tow paths and town streets
➤ LANDSCAPE	Roman wall, 19th-century waterways, 21st-century wheel
➤ SUGGESTED MAPS	OS Explorer 349 Falkirk, Cumbernauld & Livingston
➤ START/FINISH	Grid reference: NS 868800
➤ DOG FRIENDLINESS	Good along canals
➤ PARKING	Car park at Lock 16, by Union Inn
➤ PUBLIC TOILETS	At Falkirk Wheel Visitor Centre

walk directions

1 Start at the Union Inn by Lock 16. This was once one of the best-known pubs in Scotland and catered for passengers on the canal. Turn right now, away from the canal, then go right along the road. Turn right along Tamfourhill Road and go through the kissing gate on the left-hand side of the road. Alternatively, don't turn up Tamfourhill Road yet, but continue walking uphill to go under the viaduct. Keep walking all the way up until you come to a monument on the left. This commemorates the Battle of Falkirk (1298) in which William Wallace was beaten by Edward I's troops. Retrace your steps, under the viaduct, turn left into Tamfourhill Road, and left through the kissing gate on the left-hand side of the road.

2 This takes you to a section of the Roman Antonine Wall – there's a deep ditch and a rampart behind it. Walk along here, going parallel with Tamfourhill Road. When you reach the point where you can go no further, climb up the bank on the right-hand side and go down the steps to join the road by a kissing gate.

3 Go left to continue along the road – you'll soon see another kissing gate on the left leading you to another, much shorter, section of the wall. Leave the wall, rejoin the road and maintain direction to reach a mini-roundabout. Turn left here, along Maryfield Place. When you reach the end, join the public footpath signed to the canal tow path and woodland walks. Follow this track as it winds up and over the railway bridge, then on to reach the Union Canal.

4 Don't cross the canal but turn right and walk along the tow path. This is a long straight stretch now, popular with local joggers. Eventually you'll reach Roughcastle tunnel – but remember that it currently closes at 6pm to protect the Wheel from the risk of vandalism.

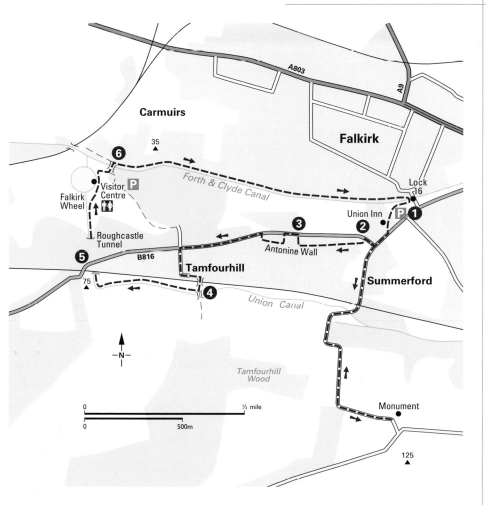

5 Walk through the tunnel – it's bright and clean and dry. This will bring you out to the new Falkirk Wheel (and yet another section of the Antonine Wall). You can walk on as far as the Wheel, then walk down to the visitor centre at the bottom. Bear right from here to cross the little bridge over the Forth and Clyde Canal.

6 Turn right now and walk along the tow path. Lots of dog walkers and cyclists come along here (so take care if you are walking with a dog), while people frequently go canoeing along the canal. Keep walking until you come back to Lock 16, then turn right and cross the canal again to return to the start of the walk at the Union Inn.

*A refreshing walk
along the cliffs to see
some local wildife.*

A Windy Walk to St Abb's Head

S t Abb's Head is one of those places that people forget to visit. You only ever seem to hear it mentioned on the shipping forecast – and its name is generally followed by a rather chilly outlook – along the lines of 'north-easterly five, continuous light drizzle, poor'. In fact you could be forgiven for wondering if it even exists or is simply a mysterious expanse of sea – like Dogger, Fisher or German Bight.

*ABOVE: The lighthouse at St Abb's Head
LEFT: Houses and cliffs surround the
harbour at St Abbs*

But St Abb's Head does exist, as you'll find out on this lovely windswept walk which will rumple your hair and leave the salty tang of the sea lingering on your lips. The dramatic cliffs, along which you walk to reach the lonely lighthouse, form an ideal home for thousands of nesting seabirds as they provide superb protection from mammalian predators. Birds you might spot on this walk include guillemots, razorbills, kittiwakes, herring gulls, shags and fulmars – as well as a few puffins. Guillemots and razorbills are difficult to differentiate, as they're both black and white, and have an upright stance – rather like small, perky penguins. However, you should be able to spot the difference if you've got binoculars as razorbills have distinctive blunt beaks. Both birds belong to the auk family, the most famous member of which is probably the great auk, which went the way of the dodo and became extinct in 1844 – a victim of the contemporary passion for egg collecting.

Nesting on Cliffs and Rocks

Luckily no egg collector could scale these cliffs, which are precipitous and surrounded by treacherous seas. Do this walk in the nesting season (May to July) and you may well see young birds jumping off the high cliff ledge into the open sea below. Even though they can't yet fly, as their wings are little more than stubs, the baby birds are nevertheless excellent swimmers and have a better chance of survival in the water than in their nests – where they could fall prey to marauding gulls. Neither razorbills nor guillemots are particularly agile in the air, but they swim with the ease of seals, using their wings and feet to propel and steer their sleek little bodies as they fish beneath the waves.

While the steep cliffs are home to most of the seabirds round St Abb's Head, the low, flat rocks below are also used by wildlife, as they are the favoured nesting site of shags. These large black birds are almost indistinguishable from cormorants – except for the distinctive crest on their heads that gives them a quizzical appearance. They tend to fly low over the water, in contrast to the graceful fulmars that frequently soar along the cliff tops as you walk, hitching a ride on convenient currents of air.

walk information

➤ **DISTANCE**	4 miles (6.4km)
➤ **MINIMUM TIME**	1hr 30min
➤ **ASCENT/GRADIENT**	443ft (135m) ▲▲▲
➤ **LEVEL OF DIFFICULTY**	🚶🚶🚶
➤ **PATHS**	Clear footpaths and established tracks
➤ **LANDSCAPE**	Dramatic cliff tops and lonely lighthouse
➤ **SUGGESTED MAPS**	OS Explorer 346 Berwick-upon-Tweed
➤ **START/FINISH**	Grid reference: NT 913674
➤ **DOG FRIENDLINESS**	They'll love the fresh air, but keep on lead by cliffs
➤ **PARKING**	At visitor centre
➤ **PUBLIC TOILETS**	At visitor centre

walk directions

1 From the car park, take the path that runs past the information board and the play area. Walk past the visitor centre, then take the footpath on the left, parallel to the main road. At the end of the path turn left and go through a gate – you'll immediately get great views of the sea.

2 Follow the track, pass the sign to Starney Bay and continue, passing fields on your left-hand side. Your track now winds around the edge of the bay – to your right is the little harbour at St Abbs. The track then winds around the cliff edge, past dramatic rock formations and eventually to some steps.

LEFT: *Seagulls rest on rocks near St Abb's Head*

3 Walk down the steps, then follow the grassy track as it bears left, with a fence on the left. Go up a slope, through a gate and maintain direction on the obvious grassy track. The path soon veers away from the cliff edge, past high ground on the right, then runs up a short, steep slope to a crossing of tracks, passing a butterfly haven on the right.

4 Maintain direction by keeping to the coastal path which runs up a slope. You'll soon get great views of the St Abb's lighthouse ahead, dramatically situated on the cliff's edge. Continue to the lighthouse and walk in front of the lighthouse buildings and down to join a tarmac road. Take care as this path is steep and eroded.

5 Follow the road down to the bottom of the hill, then 50yds (46m) before a cattle grid, turn left down a narrow path.

6 Continue along the path and over a stile. The path now runs through scrub and woodland along the edge of a loch. Continue along the path to an intersection with a track.

7 Turn right along the wide track and walk up to the road. Go left now and continue to cross a cattle grid. When you reach a bend in the road, follow the tarmac track as it bears left. You'll soon go through a gate, then pass some cottages before reaching the car park on the left-hand side.

Extending the Walk

You can add a different dimension to your walk in this area by visiting the priory ruins in Coldingham. From the harbour in St Abbs, head south along the coastal footpath towards Coldingham Bay. A lane will take you up into the village where you can visit the priory. Return to St Abbs by following the main road until you reach the Creel Road path on your right. This will take you down into the back of St Abbs, above the harbour.

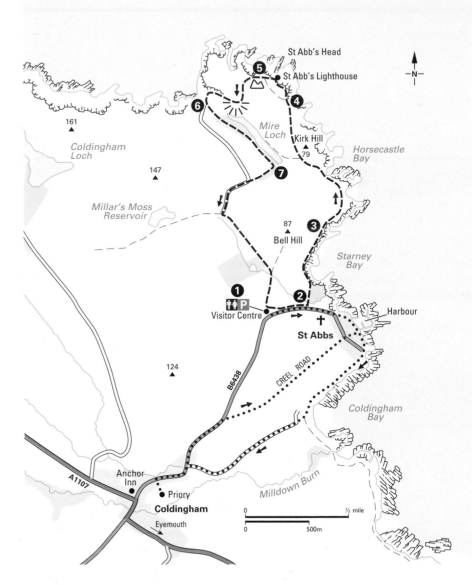

RIGHT: The rocky headland of St Abb's Head Nature Reserve

*A rustic walk from a model
industrial community.*

A Revolutionary Utopia at New Lanark

ABOVE: *The Counting House, New Lanark*
LEFT: *The Spinning Mill's New Buildings on the
banks of the River Clyde*

*… I know that society may be formed so as to exist without
crime, without poverty, with health greatly improved, with
little, if any misery, and with intelligence and happiness
increased a hundredfold…*

Robert Owen, from a speech made in 1816

I f you do this walk you'll get a glimpse of
Utopia, for the planned industrial village of
New Lanark was the embodiment of one
man's vision of an ideal world. New Lanark
was built as a cotton spinning centre in 1785
by David Dale and Richard Arkwright, and is
so well preserved that it is now a UNESCO
World Heritage Site. It owes its fame to Dale's
son-in-law, Robert Owen, who took over its
management in 1798 and made it the focus of
a revolutionary social experiment.

Forward-thinking Pioneer

Owen was a very efficient businessman and ran a strict regime, monitoring wages, insisting on good timekeeping and dismissing employees for persistent drunkenness and theft. His methods made New Lanark extremely profitable. He was also an extremely fair employer and New Lanark was no 'dark satanic mill'.

Owen believed in humane capitalism and felt that businesses were more successful if the workers were well treated. Unlike most industrialists of his day, he did not allow children under the age of ten to work in his mills, and he established the world's first nursery school. He also ensured that all children received a rounded education: by the age of seven they were attending lessons on everything from history and geography to nature study and dancing. Education didn't end when the children began working in the mills, for all his employees were encouraged to attend evening classes, lectures and dancing classes in the wonderfully named Institute for the Formation of Character. Owen also disapproved of the cruel treatment of his workers and refused to allow corporal punishment to be used as a form of discipline. His staff were provided with good housing, free medical care and a co-operative store.

Owen tried hard to persuade other industrialists to adopt his caring regime, but failed. Disillusioned, he sold New Lanark in 1825 and travelled to America where he bought a settlement in Indiana, which he named New Harmony. He intended to turn it into a Utopian community, freed from the strictures of 19th-century Britain. The experiment did not work as well as he hoped and he returned to Britain in 1828, where he continued to campaign for workers' welfare, even leading a march protesting against the plight of the Tolpuddle Martyrs, six men who were transported for seven years for forming a trade union. Owen died in 1858. He never managed to create Utopia, but inspired several other model villages such as Saltaire, Port Sunlight and Bournville, and influenced attitudes for years to come.

TOP RIGHT: Looking down on the Spinning Mill's New Buildings

walk directions

1 From the car park, walk downhill into New Lanark. Bear left and walk to the Scottish Wildlife Trust visitor centre. Turn up the stone steps on the left, following the signs to the Falls of Clyde. The path soon goes down some steps to reach the weir, where there's a lookout point.

2 Continue along the path. You'll pass Bonnington Power Station on your right, where it divides. Take the right-hand path, which takes you into woodland and up some steps. You'll soon come to Corra Linn waterfall, with another lookout point.

3 Your path continues to the right, signposted 'Bonnington Linn, 0.75 miles'. Go up some more steps and follow the track to go under a double line of pylons. Follow the path to reach the weir, cross it, then turn right into the Wildlife Reserve.

4 After 100yds (91m), turn right off the track down a narrow path, which crosses a footbridge and then follows the river, rejoining the main path downstream. Bear right here to reach Corra Castle. Continue walking by the river, cross a small footbridge, then follow the wide path through the woods. When you meet another path, turn right.

5 Follow the path to pass houses on your left. At the road turn right, then right again to cross the old bridge, which brings you into a cul de sac. Go through the gate on the right – it looks like someone's drive but is part of the Clyde Walkway.

6 Walk past the stables, then turn left through a gate to follow the riverside path. Beyond another gate, continue up some steps beside a water treatment plant and bear right along a tarmac lane. Follow the lane past some houses until you see a sign to Jooker's Johnnie on your left. Just 20yds (18m) further on, turn right down a driveway, then right again at a sign for the Clyde Walkway.

7 Your path zig-zags down to the river. At the water's edge turn left, and follow the forest track back to New Lanark. When the path meets the road turn right, then left at the church for the car park.

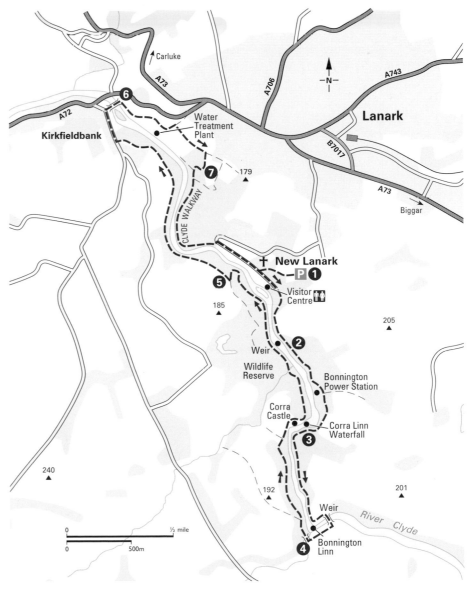

walk information

➤ **DISTANCE**	6.5 miles (10.4km)
➤ **MINIMUM TIME**	3hrs
➤ **ASCENT/GRADIENT**	476ft (145m) ▲▲▲
➤ **LEVEL OF DIFFICULTY**	👤👤👤
➤ **PATHS**	Clear riverside tracks and forest paths, a few steep steps
➤ **LANDSCAPE**	Planned industrial town and some stunning waterfalls
➤ **SUGGESTED MAPS**	OS Explorer 335 Lanark & Tinto Hills
➤ **START/FINISH**	Grid reference: NS 883426
➤ **DOG FRIENDLINESS**	Mostly off lead
➤ **PARKING**	Main car park above New Lanark
➤ **PUBLIC TOILETS**	Visitor centre, when open

*There are reminders of the
founders of an encyclopaedia
on this lovely walk.*

A Reference to Peebles

Next time you're watching University Challenge, listening to Brain of Britain, or even taking part in your local pub quiz night, think for a moment about the person who has compiled the questions. They've almost certainly come up with some of them after referring to an encyclopaedia. We tend to take these great tomes for granted, casually assuming that everything they say is correct, often giving little thought to the people that produce them.

*ABOVE: Neidpath Castle
overlooking the River Tweed
LEFT: Neidpath Castle was built
in the 14th century*

This walk starts and finishes in Peebles – the birthplace of the Chambers brothers, the founding publishers of the famous *Chambers' Encyclopaedia*.William, the older brother, was born in 1800 and in 1814 was apprenticed to a bookseller in Edinburgh. Robert, born in 1802, later followed him to the city and in 1819 they set up in business as booksellers, then branched out into printing as well. They seemed to have a flair for the trade and, in 1832, William started *Chambers' Edinburgh Journal*, a publication to which Robert contributed many essays. It was a success and later that year the brothers established the publishing house W & R Chambers. Robert, who seemed to be the more literary of the two, continued to write in his spare time and in 1844 anonymously published a book with the less-than-catchy title *Vestiges of the Natural History of Creation*. It was a controversial work, dealing with issues that were then considered blasphemy. Charles Darwin later praised it, saying it had helped to prepare the ground for his book *On the Origin of Species* (1859).

An Encyclopaedia is Born

The first edition of the *Chambers' Encyclopaedia* (1859–68) encompassed ten volumes and was edited by Robert. It was based on a translation of a German work. Robert, who had become friendly with Sir Walter Scott, continued to write, producing books on a wide range of subjects such as history, literature and geology. He also wrote a reference work entitled *A Biographical Dictionary of Eminent Scotsmen* (1832–34).

Although not as prolific as his brother, William, too, wrote a number of books, including a *History of Peeblesshire*, which came out in 1864. He did not forget his origins in Peebles and in 1859 he founded and endowed a museum, library and art gallery in the town. It's still there today, on the High Street, and is worth visiting, if only for an enormous frieze – a copy of the Elgin marbles that were taken from the Parthenon in Athens and are now in the British Museum. When the brothers died, Robert in 1871 and William in 1883, the company was taken over by Robert's son. The name Chambers is still associated with scholarly reference works today.

RIGHT: The Chambers Institute in Peebles
FAR RIGHT: Peebles' Parish Church

walk information

➤ **DISTANCE**	3.5 miles (5.7km)
➤ **MINIMUM TIME**	1hr 20min
➤ **ASCENT/GRADIENT**	295ft (90m) ▲▲▲
➤ **LEVEL OF DIFFICULTY**	🚶🚶🚶
➤ **PATHS**	Waymarked riverside paths and metalled tracks
➤ **LANDSCAPE**	Rolling borderlands and Tweed Valley
➤ **SUGGESTED MAPS**	OS Explorer 337 Peebles & Innerleithen
➤ **START/FINISH**	Grid reference: NT 250402
➤ **DOG FRIENDLINESS**	Great, chance to swim in the river
➤ **PARKING**	Kingsmeadows Road car park, Peebles
➤ **PUBLIC TOILETS**	At car park

walk directions

1 From Kingsmeadows car park, turn right and cross the bridge. Turn left at the Bridge Hotel and walk down the slope, past the swimming pool, to the river. Cross a small footbridge, go up some steps, turn left, descend some steps and follow the riverside track to pass a metal bridge and a children's play area.

2 Continue following the obvious path and go over a little bridge over a burn, after which the path becomes a little more rugged. You now enter the woods, via a gate. Eventually you leave the woods and come to the medieval, romantic-looking Neidpath Castle on the right-hand side.

3 From the castle continue walking by the river to go through another gate. You'll soon come on to higher ground and will get a great view of the old railway bridge spanning the water in front of you. After another kissing gate, maintain your direction to reach the red sandstone bridge.

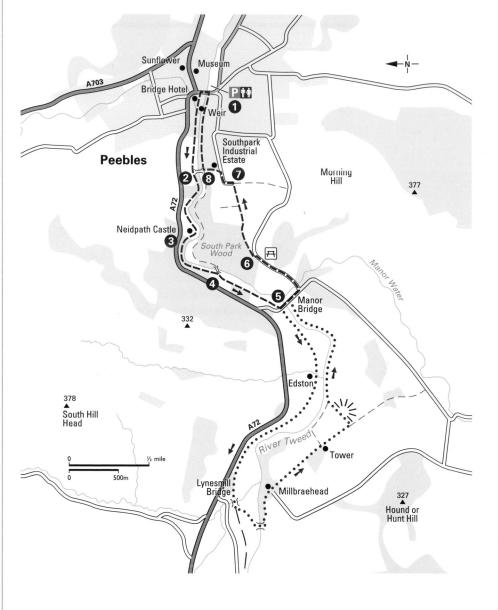

Sunflower　Museum

A703

Bridge Hotel

P　①

Weir

Peebles

Southpark
Industrial
Estate

②　⑧　⑦

Morning
Hill

377

A72

Neidpath Castle

③

*South Park
Wood*

⑥

④

⑤

Manor
Bridge

332

Manor Water

378
South Hill
Head

Edston

327
Hound or
Hunt Hill

A72

River Tweed

Tower

0 　　　　 ½ mile

0 　　 500m

Lynesmill
Bridge

Millbraehead

4 Go up to the right of the bridge, so that you join the old railway line – you now maintain direction and continue following the Tweed Walk. Follow along this disused track until you you find yourself at another attractive bridge – Manor Bridge.

5 Turn left here and cross the bridge, then take the turning on the left signed 'Tweed Walk'. You're now on a quiet lane that winds uphill – do stop and look behind you for classic views of the Borders landscape, with lush rolling hills and the wide, busy Tweed. Continue until you reach a track on the left that leads into the woods, opposite a picnic site.

6 Follow this path uphill, parallel to the road. Just before the path rejoins the road, continue down a wide, grassy path signposted to Peebles, with trees to the left. Beyond a gate, the path runs through fields until you join a tarmac road.

7 Follow this road and turn left beyond the Southpark Garage into Southpark Industrial Estate, following signs to Riverside Path. Walk between the units, then go down some steps and bear left when you reach the bottom. You'll soon reach a footbridge ahead of you.

8 Turn right here and follow the wide track beside the river. This is a popular part of the walk and attracts lots of families on sunny days. Continue walking past the weir, then go up the steps at the bridge and cross over to return to the car park.

Extending the Walk

A riverside extension adds 3.5 miles (5.7km) to this walk. Instead of crossing Manor Bridge, carry on along the banks of the Tweed to Lynesmill Bridge. You can cross an old railway bridge here then ascend the hillside on the opposite bank for some fine views. Obvious paths will lead you back down to the other side of Manor Bridge where you can resume the main walk back into Peebles from Point 5.

Follow waymarked footpaths

from this historic town.

Holy Orders at Jedburgh

ABOVE: *Monteviot House in Jedburgh*

Although it was built back in the 12th century, the beauty and grandeur of Jedburgh Abbey is still clearly evident. It certainly dominates this bustling border town, and sits serene and seemingly untroubled by the hustle and hassle of modern life. It must have seemed still more impressive in medieval times, when the power of the Church was at its height and the population was generally uneducated and superstitious.

The abbey is one of four in the Borders – the others being at Dryburgh, Kelso and Melrose – and all were built after the Norman Conquest. They are stretched across the Borders like a string of ecclesiastical jewels. Jedburgh Abbey is one of the most impressive medieval buildings in Scotland. It was built for French Augustinian canons in 1138 by David I, on the site of an earlier Anglo-Saxon monastery, and was specifically designed to make a visual impact. This was not because the King was exceedingly devout, but was due to the fact that Jedburgh is very close to the border with England. David needed to make an obvious statement of authority to his powerful Norman neighbours.

Monastic Life

Each of the Border abbeys belonged to a different religious order. The Augustinian canons at Jedburgh were also known as 'Black Canons' owing to the colour of their robes. Unlike monks, canons were all ordained clergymen who were allowed to administer Holy Communion. Dryburgh Abbey was founded by Premonstratensian canons, who wore white robes and lived a more secluded life than the Augustinians. Kelso Abbey, which became one of the largest monasteries in Scotland, belonged to the Benedictine order, while Melrose was founded by Cistercian monks. The Cistercians took their name from the forest of Cîteaux in France, where their first community was established. Often known as 'White Benedictines', Cistercian monks adhered strictly to the Rule of St Benedict. Manual labour in the abbey was carried out by poor, and generally illiterate, lay brothers. These people lived and worshipped separately to the 'choir' monks who devoted their time to reading, writing and private prayer. The Cistercians adhered to a strict regime, designed to purify their lives. They banned the use of practical goods such as bedspreads, combs and even underwear.

Abbeys Under Fire

These medieval abbeys all suffered in the battles that ravaged the Borders for centuries. Jedburgh, for example, was stripped of its roofing lead by Edward I's troops who stayed here during the Wars of Independence. It came under attack many times and was burned by the Earl of Surrey in 1530. After the Reformation, all the abbeys fell into decline and began to decay. Today they remain picturesque reminders of a previous age.

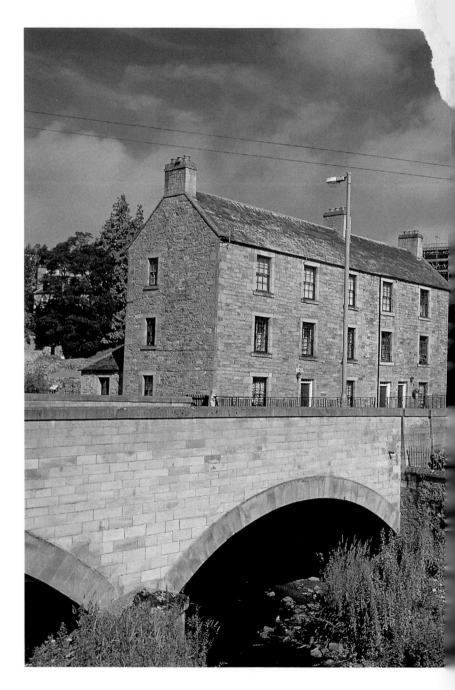

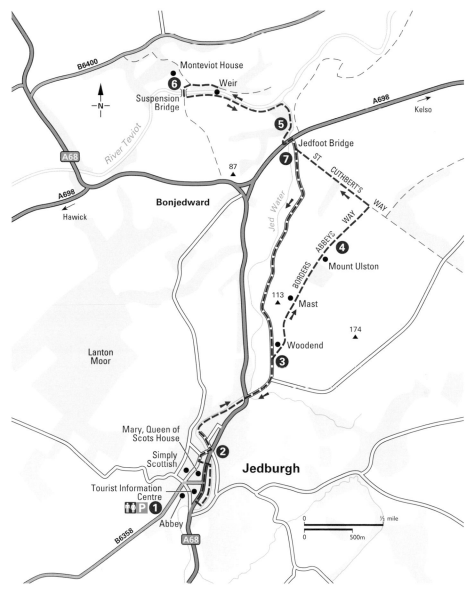

LEFT: A bridge over the River Jed leads to the roofless Jedburgh Abbey

walk directions

1 From the car park, walk back to the A68. Cross the road into Duck Row. Take the path on the left to walk beside the river, under an old bridge, then come on to the road. Turn right across the bridge.

2 Turn left, following the sign for Borders Abbeys Way. Where the road divides, turn left and follow the lane beside a builders' yard to join 'Waterside Walk'. When you reach the main road, cross and follow the tarmac lane uphill. Keep straight on, passing a turning on the right, until you reach a fork, just before a farmyard development on the left.

3 Turn right here to walk in front of a small farmhouse called Woodend. Turn left on to a footpath and continue past the front of Mount Ulston house. Your route now runs uphill, taking you past a radio mast. Maintain direction to join the narrow grassy track – this can get very muddy, even in the summer.

4 Continue along this track until you reach the fingerpost at the end, where you turn left to join St Cuthbert's Way. The going becomes much easier now as you are walking along a wide, firm track. When you reach the tarmac road, turn right and join the main road. Turn left, go over the bridge, then cross the road. Hop over the crash barrier and go down some steps to continue following St Cuthbert's Way.

walk information

➤ **DISTANCE**	4.5 miles (7.2km)
➤ **MINIMUM TIME**	3hrs
➤ **ASCENT/GRADIENT**	295ft (90m) ▲▲▲
➤ **LEVEL OF DIFFICULTY**	🚶🚶🚶
➤ **PATHS**	Tracks, meadow paths and some sections of road, 2 stiles
➤ **LANDSCAPE**	Gentle hills and fine old abbey
➤ **SUGGESTED MAPS**	OS Explorer OL16 The Cheviot Hills
➤ **START/FINISH**	Grid reference: NT 651204
➤ **DOG FRIENDLINESS**	Fair, but keep on lead near sheep and on road
➤ **PARKING**	Main car park by tourist information centre
➤ **PUBLIC TOILETS**	At car park

5 You're now on a narrow, grassy track, which runs beside the river. You then have to nip over a couple of stiles, before walking across a meadow frequently grazed by sheep. Walk past the weir, then go through the gate to cross the suspension bridge – take care as it can get extremely slippery here.

6 You now pass a sign for Monteviot House and walk through the woods to reach a fingerpost, where you can turn right to enjoy views over the river. If you wish to extend your walk, you can continue along St Cuthbert's Way until it joins the road, then retrace your steps. Whatever you choose, you then retrace your steps back over the suspension bridge, along the riverside and back to the main road. Turn left across a bridge, then immediately right down a tarmac lane.

7 Ignoring the track off to the left, follow the road all the way back to Jedburgh. Cross the A68 and return back along 'Waterside Walk' to the car park.

RIGHT: Mary, Queen of Scots House in Jedburgh
LEFT: The ruins of Jedburgh Abbey

*A ramble taking in an
ancient fortress and a
National Nature Reserve.*

Caerlaverock Castle and the
Solway Merses

Against the impressive backdrop of
Criffel, guarded by the wide waters of
the Solway Firth, the salt marshes and
the impressive medieval castle of Caerlaverock,
this out-of-the-way corner of Scotland is a haven
for wildlife and a treasure trove of history.

*ABOVE: A memorial to Sir Peter Scott
LEFT: Caerlaverock Castle*

A Castle Under Siege

Caerlaverock, the Castle of the Lark, was once the main gatekeeper to south-west Scotland. Protected by mudflats and the shifting channels of the sea, it was vulnerable only from the landward side. During the Scottish Wars of Independence (1286–1370) it was attacked frequently. From the siege of Caerlaverock by Edward I in 1300 through to the 17th century it was continually beseiged, levelled and rebuilt. Its garrison last surrendered in 1640. Partially demolished, it crumbled to an ivy-covered ruin until restoration began in the mid-20th century.

Preserving the Balance

Conservation work of a different kind takes place on the merse (salt marsh) that bounds the Solway coast. Here Scottish Natural Heritage (SNH), the Wildfowl and Wetlands Trust (WWT) and the Caerlaverock Estate work at preserving the delicate balance that allows farming and wild fowling to exist alongside a National Nature Reserve. The desolate open spaces, unchanged for centuries, echo to the cry of the wild geese in winter, the oystercatcher and heron in summer and the mating chorus of the natterjack toad in spring. But it wasn't always so. Wildfowling had seriously reduced the goose population to a few hundred in 1957, when the local landowner, the Duke of Norfolk, agreed to divide the merse into an area for controlled shooting and a wildlife sanctuary, now the National Nature Reserve. This is also one of the last places in Britain where scientists can study the important natural processes of growth and erosion of salt marshes.

Sir Peter Scott

In 1970 the Duke offered the naturalist, Sir Peter Scott, the lease of Eastpark Farm for the WWT. Every October, the Spitsbergen population of barnacle geese fly in from Norway to their winter quarters along the merse. The birds can be seen from hides shielded with high hedges to minimise disturbance to wildlife. Whooper swans overwinter here, too, along with the pink-footed goose, pintail, scaup, oystercatcher, knot, bar-tailed godwit, curlew and redshank. Staff organise events to help visitors appreciate the reserve, including birding, natterjack toad and bat spotting, and pond dipping. As part of the conservation process, wildfowling is permitted in winter. Barnacle geese are protected but other species are fair game. The wildfowlers are experts at recognition and SNH wardens ensure fair play.

walk information

➤ **DISTANCE**	5.25 miles (8.4km)
➤ **MINIMUM TIME**	2hrs 30min
➤ **ASCENT/GRADIENT**	82ft (25m) ▲▲▲
➤ **LEVEL OF DIFFICULTY**	🐾🐾🐾
➤ **PATHS**	Country lanes, farm tracks and salt marsh, 1 stile
➤ **LANDSCAPE**	Pastures, salt marsh, riverside and hills
➤ **SUGGESTED MAPS**	OS Explorer 314 Solway Firth
➤ **START/FINISH**	Grid reference: NY 051656
➤ **DOG FRIENDLINESS**	Keep on lead while on reserve
➤ **PARKING**	Car park at Wildfowl and Wetlands Trust Reserve
➤ **PUBLIC TOILETS**	At Wildfowl and Wetlands Trust Reserve

walk directions

1 Exit the car park and turn right on to a farm road. Follow this past the farms of Newfield and Midtown then turn left and go past a bungalow and some houses. Just before the farm of Hollands there is a waymarker pointing to a car park, on the right, and straight ahead for walks. Go straight ahead and continue to the farm steading, then turn left.

2 Go through a gate and on to a farm track. This stretches away into the distance and has high hedges on both sides. Continue along this track between the hedges and on, over an overgrown section, until you reach the end then turn right at the signpost indicating Caerlaverock.

3 A sign here informs visitors that regulated wildfowling (shooting) takes place between 1 September to 20 February. Follow the rough track through the grass along the edge of the merse in the direction of the arrow on the

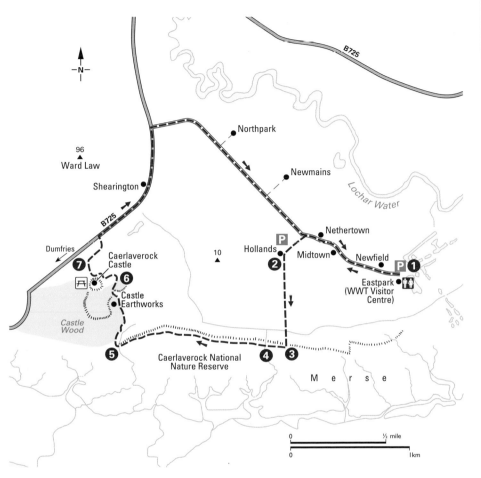

footpath waymarker post. The path can be very boggy at all times and the grass will be high in the summer.

4 The path through the nature reserve varies from faint to non-existent; Wellington boots are recommended. It splits at several points and then meanders back and forth, but all the lines of the path rejoin and you'll end up at the same place whichever one you decide to take.

5 Eventually some cottages can be seen in the field to the right. Bear right, through a gate and into the field. Walk to the left around the field perimeter, past some cottages, then turn left through a gate to emerge on to a farm track, passing a sign for Caerlaverock Castle and into the castle grounds.

6 Follow the road past the old castle, which has been excavated and has information boards to explain the ruins, and go through a wood with nature trail information boards to Caerlaverock Castle. There is a children's playground, a siege machine and picnic tables around the ramparts of the castle.

7 At the far end go through an arch and continue to the T-junction with a country lane. Turn right and continue for about a mile (1.6km), then turn right on to another lane signposted 'Wildfowl and Wetlands Reserve'. Continue on this road past the farms of Northpark, Newmains and Nethertown and then back to the car park at Eastpark.

ABOVE LEFT: A tower at Caerlaverock Castle

*An exhilarating climb is followed
by a more gentle stroll past
Hugh MacDiarmid's memorial.*

A Poet's Passions at Langholm

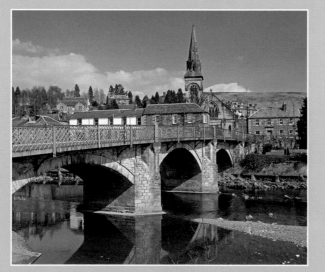

The Scots have long been passionate about their independence and take great pride in their rich culture. On this walk you'll pass a memorial to one of the founding fathers of the modern Scottish nationalist movement – the poet Hugh MacDiarmid.

*ABOVE: A bridge spans the River Esk in Langholm
LEFT: A bench overlooking superb
countryside at Langholm*

A Cultural Giant

MacDiarmid (real name was Christopher Murray Grieve) was born in Langholm in 1892 and is considered one of Scotland's leading poets, and deserves to rank alongside Robert Burns in cultural importance. His early working life was spent in journalism in Montrose and London, and he then turned to writing poetry. A man of passionate views – he was a communist and nationalist – his verses were written in local dialect, mixed with words taken from the older Scottish tongue. His volumes of poetry included *Sangschaw*, his first book which was published in 1925, *Penny Wheep* (1926) and *A Drunk Man Looks at the Thistle* (1926). His works sparked a renewed interest in Scottish language and culture and he became a central figure in the country's literary revival.

Championing Home Rule

During the 1930s he moved to Shetland, where he continued to write. He was once described as: 'Unmistakably the genius, with tensely thoughtful features and smouldering, deep-set eyes… (he is) almost rustically Scots… wearing a kilt and a plaid, both of bright tartan.' Years later another writer was to describe him as 'a magnificent mouse of a man'. He was by this time involved in the early nationalist movement, which had started in Scotland after the First World War. Together with other writers, such as Lewis Spence and Neil Gunn, MacDiarmid voiced a desire for Home Rule for Scotland. The movement grew into the Scottish National Party which was formed in 1934.

After the Second World War, MacDiarmid moved back to the Borders, living with his wife in a two-room labourer's cottage near Biggar. It was simple in the extreme and had no water or electricity, but it was from here that he embarked on lecture tours all over the world. He often travelled to Edinburgh, where he would meet with other Scottish writers like Norman MacCaig and Sorley MacLean.

MacDiarmid died in 1978, his love of Scotland as passionate as ever. He was buried in Langholm. Above the door of his home are inscribed the telling words:
The rose of all the world is not for me
I want for my part
Only the little white rose of Scotland
That smells sharp and sweet and breaks the heart

RIGHT: *This sculpture by Jake Harvey at Langholm is a memorial to Hugh MacDiarmid*

walk directions

1 Cross grass downstream, then go through a hedge gap on the left to pass through a small garden to the A7 above. Head into Langholm along the High Street to the post office on the left.

2 Immediately past the post office, turn left up Kirk Wynd. It becomes a tarred path, then a rough track running up to the left of the golf course to a gate. Follow the grassy path up and slightly right to reach a green seat beside Whita Well, a natural spring.

3 Now take the path to the left of the seat, running steeply up the hill. Follow it under a line of pylons and up to the top of Whita Hill. There are stone steps up to the monument, a 100ft (30m) high obelisk commemorating Sir John Malcolm, a famous soldier, diplomat and scholar.

4 From St John Malcolm's monument, walk back a few paces to join the wide gravel track that runs in front of it, then turn right. It's easy walking now, following this clear track downhill. Eventually you'll reach a metal sculpture on the left-hand side. The sculpture, which resembles an open book, was created by Jake Harvey and is a memorial to Hugh MacDiarmid.

5 Bear left past the sculpture to a small car park, and turn left. You now simply follow the road as it winds downhill – it's quite a long stretch but it's fairly quiet. Go back under the line of pylons then, just after a copse on your right-hand side, take the path on the left, signposted 'Langholm Walks 10'.

LEFT: The Malcolm Monument on Whita Hill commemorates the life of Sir John Malcolm, a renowned scholar, soldier and diplomat

walk information

➤ **DISTANCE**	3.75 miles (6km)
➤ **MINIMUM TIME**	2hrs
➤ **ASCENT/GRADIENT**	919ft (280m) ▲▲▲
➤ **LEVEL OF DIFFICULTY**	🚶🚶🚶
➤ **PATHS**	Firm hill paths and tarmac roads
➤ **LANDSCAPE**	Lush green borderlands and fine views
➤ **SUGGESTED MAPS**	OS Explorer 323 Eskdale & Castle O'er Forest
➤ **START/FINISH**	Grid reference: NY 364849
➤ **DOG FRIENDLINESS**	Keep on lead as there are plenty of sheep
➤ **PARKING**	Riverside car park (free)
➤ **PUBLIC TOILETS**	At car park and off main street of Langholm

6 Follow this footpath, slightly uphill and then above a wall, where it runs through a small boggy patch. After this you shortly return to the gate you reached on your outward journey. Turn right, through the gate, and retrace your outward route.

Extending the Walk

You can extend this walk to take in a remote section of moorland, by heading right at Point 5, the MacDiarmid memorial. Follow the road over a cattle grid and a short distance downhill to a waymarker on the right. A small path runs down towards the distant Middlemoss farm. After a footbridge over Little Tarras Water, it bends slightly right, following the reedy hollow of an older trackway. Bear left alongside a field wall, on a rough track then a path through two kissing gates, to Middlemoss's access track. Follow it left to the road, and turn left back to Point 5.

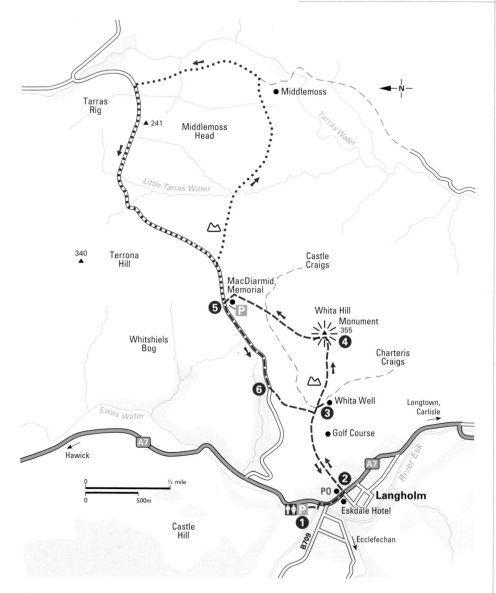

Walking in Safety

All these walks are suitable for any reasonably fit person, but less experienced walkers should try the easier walks first. Route finding is usually straightforward, but you will find that an Ordnance Survey map is a useful addition to the route maps and descriptions.

Risks

Although each walk here has been researched with a view to minimising the risks to the walkers who follow its route, no walk in the countryside can be considered to be completely free from risk. Walking in the outdoors will always require a degree of common sense and judgement to ensure that it is as safe as possible.

- Be particularly careful on cliff paths and in upland terrain, where the consequences of a slip can be very serious.
- Remember to check tidal conditions before walking on the seashore.
- Some sections of route are by, or cross, busy roads. Take care and remember traffic is a danger even on minor country lanes.
- Be careful around farmyard machinery and livestock, especially if you have children with you.
- Be aware of the consequences of changes in the weather and check the forecast before you set out. Carry spare clothing and a torch if you are walking in the winter months. Remember the weather can change very quickly at any time of the year, and in moorland and heathland areas, mist and fog can make route finding much harder. Don't set out in these conditions unless you are confident of your navigation skills in poor visibility. In summer remember to take account of the heat and sun; wear a hat and carry spare water.
- On walks away from centres of population you should carry a whistle and survival bag. If you do have an accident requiring the emergency services, make a note of your position as accurately as possible and dial 999.

Acknowledgements

The Automobile Association would like to thank the following photographers, companies and picture libraries for their assistance in the preparation of this book.

Abbreviations for the picture credits are as follows: (t) top; (b) bottom; (l) left; (r) right; (AA) AA World Travel Library.

2/3 AA S Anderson; 5 AA/J Smith; 6 AA/S Anderson; 7bl AA/S Anderson; 7bcl AA/S Whitehorne; 7bcr AA/J Smith; 7br AA/D W Robertson; 10/11 AA/S Day; 12/13 AA/R G Elliott; 13 AA; 14/15 AA/S Whitehorne; 16 AA/J Henderson; 18/19 AA/R Weir; 19 David Tipling/Alamy; 20/21 AA/K Paterson; 23 AA/K Paterson; 24 AA/J Smith; 24/25 AA/J Smith; 26/27 AA/J Smith; 29 AA/S Whitehorne; 30/31 AA/S Anderson; 31 AA/K Paterson; 32/33 AA/R Weir; 34 AA/A Baker; 36 AA/S Whitehorne; 36/37 AA/K Paterson; 40/41 AA/P Sharpe; 41 AA/J Henderson; 42/43 AA/S Anderson; 44 AA/S Day; 46 AA/R G Elliott; 46/47 AA/R Weir; 48 AA/S Day; 50/51 AA/S Day; 51 AA/J Carney; 54 AA/S Whitehorne; 54/55 AA/K Paterson; 58/59 AA/R Weir; 59 AA/A Baker; 60 AA/A Baker; 62 AA/J Smith; 63 AA/S Anderson; 64/65 AA/S Anderson; 66/67 AA/D Hardley; 68/69 AA/S Day; 69 AA/M Taylor; 70/71 AA/S Day; 71 AA/S Day; 72 AA/S Day; 74 AA/J Smith; 74/75 AA/S Whitehorne; 76 AA/J Smith; 78 AA/J Smith; 78/79 AA/J Smith; 80 AA/J Smith; 82/83 AA/M Alexander; 83 AA/J Beazley; 84/85 AA; 87 AA/J Beazley; 88 AA/S Gibson; 89 AA/S Whitehorne; 91 AA; 92/93 AA/M Taylor; 93 AA/M Taylor; 94 AA/M Alexander; 95 AA/J Henderson; 97 AA/K Paterson; 98/99 AA/J Beazley; 100 AA/S Anderson; 101 AA/S Anderson; 102/103 AA/M Alexander; 103 AA/M Alexander; 105 AA/M Alexander; 106/107 AA/R Coulam; 108/109 AA/R Coulam; 110 AA/R Coulam

Every effort has been made to trace the copyright holders, and we apologise in advance for any accidental errors. We would be happy to apply the corrections in the following edition of this publication.